PerfectMatch

Earring Designs for Every Occasion

Sara Schwittek

Cincinnati, Ohio

www.

12 11 10 09 08   5 4 3 2 1

Distributed in Canada by Fraser Direct
100 Armstrong Avenue
Georgetown, ON, Canada L7G 5S4
Tel: (905) 877-4411

Distributed in the U.K. and Europe by David & Charles
Brunel House, Newton Abbot, Devon, TQ12 4PU, England
Tel: (+44) 1626 323200, Fax: (+44) 1626 323319
E-mail: postmaster@davidandcharles.co.uk

Distributed in Australia by Capricorn Link
P.O. Box 704, S. Windsor, NSW 2756 Australia
Tel: (02) 4577-3555

Library of Congress Cataloging-in-Publication Data
Schwittek, Sara.
  Perfect match : earring designs for every occasion / by Sara Schwittek. -- 1st ed.
    p. cm.
  Includes index.
  ISBN 978-1-60061-068-4 (pbk. : alk. paper)
  1. Jewelry making. 2. Earrings. I. Title.
TT212.S43 2008
739.27--dc22
                          2007046996

fw
F+W PUBLICATIONS, INC.
www.fwpublications.com

Editor: Robin M. Hampton
Designer: Cheryl Mathauer, Corrie Schaffeld
Production Coordinator: Greg Nock
Photographers: John Carrico, Alias Imaging LLC, Tim Grondin
Photo Stylist: Lauren Emmerling

Metric Conversion Chart

TO CONVERT	TO	MULTIPLY BY
Inches	Centimeters	2.54
Centimeters	Inches	0.4
Feet	Centimeters	30.5
Centimeters	Feet	0.03
Yards	Meters	0.9
Meters	Yards	1.1
Sq. Inches	Sq. Centimeters	6.45
Sq. Centimeters	Sq. Inches	0.16
Sq. Feet	Sq. Meters	0.09
Sq. Meters	Sq. Feet	10.8
Sq. Yards	Sq. Meters	0.8
Sq. Meters	Sq. Yards	1.2
Pounds	Kilograms	0.45
Kilograms	Pounds	2.2
Ounces	Grams	28.3
Grams	Ounces	0.035

Dedication

This book is dedicated to my very first best friend, my twin sister, Amy. My whole life you've been there with me: laughing, learning and being crafty. I think we make a "perfect match"!

Acknowledgments

A big thank you to my editor, Robin Hampton, my patient photographer, Tim Grondin, and my talented designers, Cheryl Mathauer and Corrie Schaffeld. Also, a huge thank you to Jessica Gordon for giving me the opportunity to go on this adventure.

Of course, thanks go to my husband, Michael, who always forgives me for the miscellaneous wire clippings, headpins and stray beads found in the bed.

About the author

Sara Schwittek is one of the creators of Shy Siren, a line of stunning jewelry handcrafted with semiprecious gemstones, pearls, crystals and glass beads. Sara started as an architectural designer in New York City. She left architecture to launch Four Eyes, a Web design studio, with her husband, Michael. Sara's diverse background in all-things-design gives her a unique lens through which to view the world of jewelry. Sara creates each piece with an eye toward both aesthetics and functionality, taking pleasure in the play of light and colors of the materials she works with. She also enjoys photography, yoga and, more recently, learning how to sew. You can see more of her work online at www.perfectmatchearrings.com or her online shop at www.shysiren.com.

Around the World (page 54)

contents

Mirror, Mirror Hoops (page 96)

Introduction:

SmallProjects, BigRewards

"Where did you get those earrings?!" You'll love hearing it over and over when people stop to admire your new baubles. It's so fun, easy, fast and inexpensive to make incredible earrings. With just a little free time, some basic skills and tools and a few beautiful beads, you'll have dazzling earrings and endless possibilities for perfect hand-made gifts for your friends and family.

Earrings show off your personal taste. You may like petite earrings that subtly accentuate your face or your outfit. Or you might take an opposite approach and decide on the earrings first and then pick out the outfit! This book is organized into social occasions with a series of fashionable, fun earrings in a variety of styles for each situation. If you're heading for a big night out, you'll want to check out the flashy designs in the Night on the Town chapter (page 142). Before meeting up with friends for dim sum this weekend, check out the Sunday Brunch with Friends chapter (page 106).

You probably have a busy schedule to balance among your work, family and friends. Most of the earrings in this book can be made with just a little spare time and some inspiration. Take a glance at clocks on the opening page of each design to quickly see how much time you need to complete the earrings, whether it's fifteen, thirty or sixty minutes. And, right under the clocks you'll find the length of the finished earrings.

With just the basic skills found in the Techniques for Making Earrings section (page 14), you will be able to create stylish earrings that you will love wearing. Try starting with the *Timeless Crystal Earrings* (132) or the *Sea Glass Earrings* (page 72) to build up your skills and confidence. If you only have a few minutes, the *Vintage Glass Bouquet Earrings* (page 86) will provide you with instant gratification! And many of the more complex earring designs are no more difficult than the simple ones—you just repeat the same technique a few more times to get the desired results. The elaborate *City Lights Crystal Earrings* (page 146), for example, use the same simple maneuvers you'll learn in the next few pages.

Most of the materials used in the earrings in this book cost less than the price of going out to see a movie. In fact, many of the earrings cost less than your morning latte from the corner coffee shop! Yet, a classic design like *The Essential Black Earrings* (page 134) makes for an exquisite gift that will be treasured for years to come.

Perfect Match contains designs from the super-simple for beginners to the more complex for all levels of jewelry makers who are looking for inspiration. Most importantly, this book is meant to inspire you to explore the possibilities of this extremely versatile accessory! Feel free to substitute your favorite colors or materials when creating the projects in this book. Let the featured earring designs whet your appetite, and open your imagination to all the possibilities!

WhatYouNeedToStart

Doesn't your mouth water and your heart beat faster when you walk into a bead shop? So many delicious options—your mind begins to whirl with all the possibilities! Earrings are the perfect project not only for featuring those exquisite gemstone briolettes but also for using up all those little odds and ends gathered in the bottom of your bead box. Here are a few of the items you can use, but your options are limited only by your imagination.

SEMIPRECIOUS STONES

The natural organic beauty, texture and color in these treasures from the Earth can set your pieces apart. They can range wildly in price and quality depending on their size, cut and clarity. Take into account their often irregular shapes and small-sized holes when using gemstones in your designs.

PEARLS

Freshwater pearls instantly provide a timeless, classic feel to virtually any earring design, and yet they can be surprisingly affordable. Pearls come in a wide variety of shapes—rice, potato, coin and nugget, to name a few—and are often dyed in beautiful shades of pinks, purples, blues and greens.

GLASS BEADS

Glass beads come in an endless variety of shapes, sizes and colors, and can be an inexpensive alternative to pricier gemstones and crystal. They're also very uniform in size and often have a larger hole size to accommodate thicker gauge wire or leather cording.

WOOD AND OTHER NATURAL MATERIALS

Wood, bone, shell and other natural materials can give your jewelry an earthy, organic quality. Most of these materials are inexpensive, and will give your pieces a one-of-a-kind look.

CRYSTAL BEADS

I use a lot of Swarovski crystals. These crystals are precision cut and have an unsurpassed sparkle. They're available in a huge variety of gorgeous colors, finishes, sizes and shapes, making them a staple in any bead library.

HEADPINS

Headpins are short pieces of wire with a flat head or a round ball at one end, often used to create dangles. Headpins come in different gauges, so test to see if they fit in the beads that you're using. 1½"–2" (4cm–5cm) lengths will meet most needs.

CHAIN

Chain is available in a wide variety of styles, sizes and finishes. Sterling silver and gold-filled chains will give your jewelry a more refined look, but gold-plated and silver-plated chains are a wonderful alternative when you need to stick to a budget. Chains also come in gunmetal, copper, brass and antiqued finishes.

SPACER BEADS

Spacer beads may not be very exciting, but they're essential in beading. Spacers provide definition to your special beads or that extra attention to detail that adds visual value to your finished piece.

EARRING HOOKS

There are so many beautiful earring hooks available at craft stores, bead shops and online. Using manufactured components can save a lot of time. However, be sure to see the techniques section (page 26) for instructions on making your own unique hooks. It's easier than you think!

DECORATIVE COMPONENTS

There are hundreds of chandeliers, connectors, charms and other decorative components available at craft and jewelry-supply stores. Be creative when it comes to components—just because it's called a "clasp" doesn't mean that you can't use it in an earring! (For designs using manufactured components, see Garden Trellis [page 118] and The Essential Black Earrings [page 134].)

If you can't find the circular or oval metal components used in some of the projects, dissect some chain and use the individual links in your designs.

Wire

When selecting wire for your projects, keep in mind the gauge and the hardness of the wire. The higher the gauge number, the thinner the wire. In all of the projects I make recommendations for what gauge wire to use, but feel free to adjust this to match the holes in your beads.

The hardness of the wire indicates how difficult it is to manipulate. Sterling silver and gold-filled wire are often available in dead-soft, half-hard and hard. I generally use half-hard, round wire.

Colored craft wire is inexpensive and comes in a rainbow of bright colors. However, it can also mar very easily, leaving unattractive dents and scratched areas. Use coated wire in projects only when the color of the wire is more important than the durability of the finished piece.

Wire Chart

WHEN YOU BUY STERLING SILVER OR GOLD-FILLED WIRE, IT'S OFTEN BY THE FOOT OR BY THE TRAY OUNCE. USE THIS HANDY CHART SO YOU KNOW HOW MUCH YOU'RE BUYING:

20 gauge = 19' (6m) per ounce
21 gauge = 25' (8m) per ounce
22 gauge = 31' (9m) per ounce
24 gauge = 48' (15m) per ounce
26 gauge = 76' (23m) per ounce
28 gauge = 120' (37m) per ounce

I use sterling silver and gold-filled wire in my projects, but while you are learning, use equal gauges of less expensive silver-plated or gold-plated brass or copper wires. You can find them at most craft stores. Plated wire will generally not be designated as soft, half-hard or hard, so you can ignore these specifications in the project instructions.

Tools

The great thing about getting started with jewelry making is that there are only a few essential tools needed to make even the most beautiful designs. Most of these basic tools can be found at your local craft store, and none of the tools need batteries or electricity!

BASIC TOOL KIT

CHAIN-NOSE PLIERS

The jaws on chain-nose pliers taper to a dull point. Use them to grip your wire while making wraps or bends. When selecting your pliers, make sure they are smooth on the inside, as textured jaws will leave marks in your wire. (Top pliers shown.)

SIDE OR FLUSH WIRE CUTTERS

Use side cutters to cut wire to size, remove excess wire from loops and wraps, and trim headpins and chains. Flush cutters leave your ends a little tidier. Buy a pair with a small, clean point so you can get into tight areas. (Middle pliers shown.)

ROUND-NOSE PLIERS

Round-nose pliers have jaws that are tapered to a point. Use them to make wire loops. Round-nose pliers with very thin jaws make smaller loops, which makes jewelry look more delicate. Mark the spot that you like on the nose with a permanent marker, so you can consistently make loops the same size. (Bottom pliers shown.)

RULER

Any ruler will work, but heavy-duty, stainless steel rulers with cork backings stay steady on work surfaces. Be sure the ruler includes both inches and centimeters, because many beads and findings are measured in millimeters.

NOTEBOOK, PEN AND COLORED PENCILS

It's always a good idea to jot down the specifics of a design that you've just created so you can reproduce it easily again in the future. You never know when you'll be hit with a jolt of inspiration for a new design or color scheme. Record it with your colored pencils!

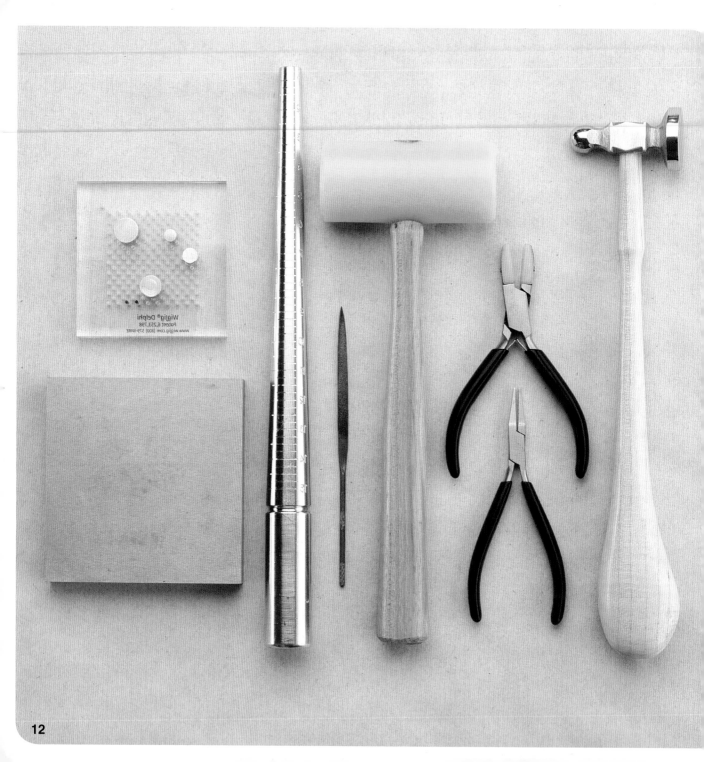

Earring Hook Tool Kit

WIRE JIG

I'd be remiss not to mention how useful a wire jig can be when you need to make lots of earring hooks with a consistent shape and size. A jig set usually comes with a plastic or metal panel with a grid of holes and corresponding pegs of varying diameters. You can wrap your wire around these pegs to shape the wire into endless forms. Making earring hooks is just the beginning of the creative things you can do with your jig.

STEEL BLOCK

Hammer on this flat, very solid surface of hardened steel to prevent damaging your work surface.

RING MANDREL

Typically used for sizing rings, you'll use a ring mandrel to form wire and create unique handmade earring hooks. As an alternative, you can use other solid objects, such as wood dowels, smooth-barreled pens, markers or other household objects, such as the round end of a lotion bottle, to achieve the same effect.

NEEDLE FILE

Use the file to smooth sharp ends of cut wire, especially when creating earring hooks. You can also use fine-grit sandpaper instead.

HARD PLASTIC MALLET

Use this tool to strike a metal object without marring or dinging it. Using this mallet ensures that the wire is not flattened. The striking action helps the metal retain its shape through the process of work-hardening (stiffening).

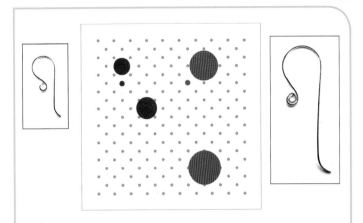

THIS DIAGRAM OF A WIRE JIG ILLUSTRATES SUGGESTED LAYOUTS OF VARIOUS SIZED PEGS TO CREATE TWO DIFFERENT STYLES OF EARRING HOOKS. SEE MORE ON PAGE 28.

NYLON-JAW PLIERS

These pliers have a plastic coating on the jaws that prevents marring on wire. Use them to straighten longer lengths of thicker wire or to work-harden the wire. (Top pliers shown.)

FLAT-NOSE PLIERS

These have a flat, squared-off tip. They have many uses, but you'll mainly use them to create wire spirals for the projects in this book. (Bottom pliers shown.)

CHASING AND BALL-PEEN HAMMER

This hammer typically has two ends: a slightly domed chasing end and a knobby ball-peen end. Use this hammer for adding textured, hammered effects in sterling silver, as well as flattening wire and other metal components.

TechniquesforMakingEarrings

There are a few basic techniques that are essential to practice before beginning. These techniques are easy to learn, and once you have the hang of them, you'll be making the pieces in *Perfect Match* in no time. Even the complex designs aren't much more difficult than the simple ones; you just need more time to repeat the same motions to get the desired results.

A few notes that apply to all projects in this book:

* Note the direction of each loop you make—parallel or perpendicular to the loop below it. You may need to adjust the direction of the loop that's attached to the earring hook so that the finished piece hangs forward.
* When you cut the tail of the wire, always tuck in any sharp edges.
* Remember to file the ends of handmade earring wires so that they are more comfortable to insert into the ear.

> I often specify a length of wire to use when wrapping a briolette or bead or when creating an earring hook. I use the minimal amount of materials to get the job done with the least amount of waste. However, while you're learning, you may find it easier to add ½"–1" (1cm–3cm) to the specifications until you get the hang of it.

STRAIGHTENING AND CLEANING YOUR WIRE

It's always best to start the project with your materials in the best possible condition. Straightening your wire not only removes some of the kinks but also work-hardens (stiffens) the wire a bit to help retain its final shape.

1. STRAIGHTEN WIRE
Hold the end of the wire with the chain-nose pliers and run the nylon-jaw pliers over the wire a few times.

2. CLEAN WIRE
Slide a silver-polishing cloth over the wire to quickly remove any tarnish on sterling silver wire. (But, don't use a cleaning cloth on plated wire; it can remove the plating.)

FILING

It's fun to create your own unique earring hooks! But when you do, it's important to smooth the sharp edges at the end of the earring hook wire.

A few pointers:

* Use a needle file to smooth the sharp edges.
* Pointing the file away from your body, slide the file against the end of the wire. File in 1 direction only.
* Rotate the wire against the file so that you are creating a dull, rounded end.

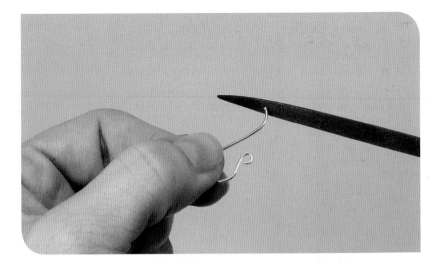

HAMMERING

There are several different types of hammers that you'll use for specific purposes in making these projects. The slightly-domed end of the chasing hammer is perfect for flattening sections of wire, such as the back of an earring hook. Add small dents and dimples to your wire and metal components with a ball-peen hammer. The light refractions from the hammered texture give your pieces an artisan quality and unique look. (Note: I don't recommend applying a hammering technique on plated metal components; it can remove the plating.) And a hard-rubber mallet is useful for work-hardening shapes you create with your wire; it won't mar or flatten the wire.

1. HAMMER WIRE OR METAL COMPONENT

Place your wire or metal component flat on your steel block on a sturdy, solid work surface. While holding onto your wire or metal components, carefully but firmly strike the object using the appropriate hammer for the effect you desire. If your piece bends up due to the hammering, hammer it flat with a hard-rubber mallet. This mallet will work-harden and flatten the piece without removing the hammered effect.

WHAT IS WORK-HARDENING?

Work-hardening is the stiffening that occurs when you bend or work with your wire. You'll want to work-harden some of your metalwork so your handmade earring hooks and other hoops retain their shape.

Hold the hammer toward the end of the handle for best control, not at the head of the hammer. I find using the steel block on a carpeted floor helps deaden the sound!

CREATING A WIRE LOOP

In this book, I often refer to "making a loop" or "begin to create a loop." There are two options for creating a loop—simple or wrapped.

Each style has its advantages, and I recommend a specific loop style in many of the projects, but feel free to do what feels right for your creations.

SIMPLE LOOP

For beginners, I recommend the simple loop. It's fast, easy to learn and can be reopened. However, its connection to other components is less secure than the wire-wrapped loop.

An advantage to using a Simple Loop is that it can be reopened and added to another chain, hoop, earring hook or loop.

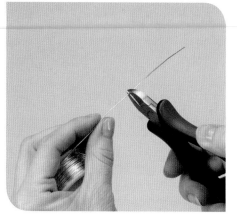

1. CUT WIRE
Using the side cutters, cut about 2" (5cm) of 24- or 26-gauge plated or copper practice wire.

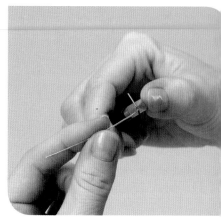

2. BEND WIRE
About ³/₈" (1cm) from the end of the wire, bend the wire 90 degrees with the chain-nose pliers.

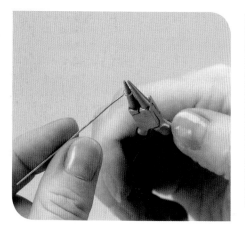

3. TURN WIRE
With the round-nose pliers, grab the short end of the wire. Turn your wrist toward your body and release the wire. Repeat until the end of the wire meets the base, forming a complete circle.

4. CLOSE GAPS
If necessary, carefully close any gaps with the chain-nose pliers. Apply gentle pressure to avoid crushing the loop.

5. OPEN LOOP (OPTIONAL)
Always twist the loop sideways with the chain-nose pliers. Never pull the circle open. When closing the loop, twist the loop sideways back to the original position.

Wire-Wrapped Loop

As your skills grow, I recommend using a wire-wrapped loop whenever possible in your designs. It provides a professional and polished look, and your jewelry will be far more durable. This loop is more time consuming and can't be reopened. However, because there are no open loops, there are fewer opportunities for pieces to come loose.

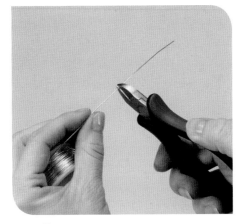

1. CUT WIRE

Using the side cutters, cut about 2–2½" (5cm–6cm) of 24- or 26-gauge plated or copper practice wire.

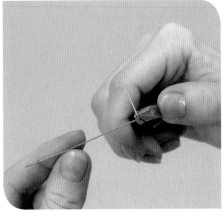

2. BEND WIRE

About 1" (3cm) from the end of the wire, bend the wire 90 degrees with the chain-nose pliers.

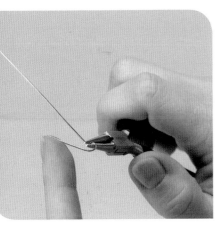

3. TURN WIRE

Position the round-nose pliers so they sit directly in the corner of the angle you made in step 2. With your fingers, press the tail of the wire around the round jaw of the round-nose pliers 1 time.

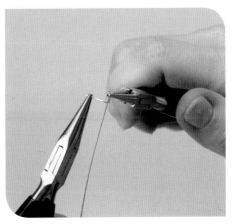

4. WRAP THE WIRE

Grab the short end of the wire with the chain-nose pliers and wrap it around the base of the loop 2 or 3 times to secure it. Release the wire and reposition your wrist and the chain-nose pliers as needed.

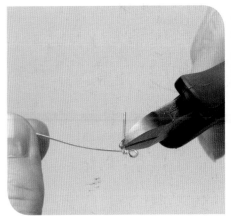

5. CUT EXCESS WIRE

Cut off the excess wire with the side cutters.

CREATING A LOOPED BEAD

Making beaded jewelry is simple—it's just a matter of completing one step, then adding the next!
To make a looped bead, start by Creating a Wire Loop: Simple Loop (page 16), then start here with step 1.

SIMPLE LOOPED BEAD

1. CREATE LOOP AND ADD BEAD
Complete steps 1-4 for Creating a Wire Loop: Simple Loop (page 16), and slide a bead onto the end of the remaining wire.

2. BEND WIRE
Bend the remaining wire 90 degrees with the chain-nose pliers in the same direction as the loop below the bead. Cut the end to about $^3/_8$" (1cm) long.

3. CREATE LOOP
With the round-nose pliers, grab the short end of the wire. Turn your wrist toward your body and release the wire. Grab the wire again and turn your wrist until the end of the wire matches up with the base in a complete circle.

4. CLOSE GAPS
If necessary, carefully close any gaps with the chain-nose pliers. Apply gentle pressure to avoid crushing the loop.

WIRE-WRAPPED LOOPED BEAD

As your skills grow, I recommend using this technique over the Simple Looped Bead (page 18) as it provides a more polished look as well as durability.

When using this technique in your designs, you will need to plan a step ahead when you're creating the loops. You'll often need to insert a chain, other closed loops or earring hooks before the loop is closed.

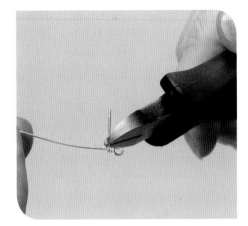

1. CREATE LOOP AND ADD BEAD
Complete steps 1–5 in Creating a Wire-Loop: Wire-Wrapped Loop (page 17). Slide a bead onto the tail of the remaining wire.

2. BEND WIRE
Leave a ⅛" (3mm) gap above the bead and bend the remaining wire 90 degrees with the chain-nose pliers in the same direction as the loop below the bead.

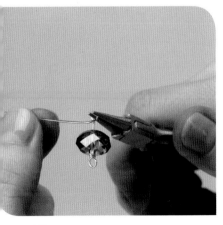

3. WRAP WIRE
Position the round-nose pliers so they sit directly in the corner of the angle you made in step 2. With your fingers, press the tail of the wire around the round jaw of the round-nose pliers 1 time.

4. WRAP WIRE AROUND BASE
Grab the short end of the wire with the chain-nose pliers and wrap it around the base of the loop 2 or 3 times to secure. Release the wire and reposition your wrist and the chain-nose pliers as needed.

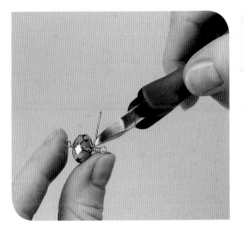

5. CUT EXCESS WIRE AND FINISH
Cut the excess wire with the side cutters. Press down any sharp edges with the chain-nose pliers.

CREATING A LOOPED DANGLE

With the basic technique that you learned in Creating a Looped Bead (pages 18–19), you can create dangles for your earrings. Again, there are two options, each with the same benefits as described in Creating a Wire Loop (pages 16–17).

SIMPLE LOOPED DANGLE

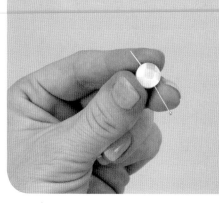

1. ADD BEADS
Slide the bead(s) onto a headpin.

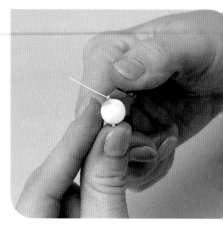

2. BEND WIRE
With the chain-nose pliers, bend the headpin wire to 90 degrees directly above the top of the bead.

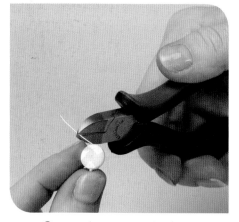

3. CUT WIRE
Cut the end of the wire to about ³⁄₈" (1cm) in length.

4. WRAP WIRE
Hold the bead in your hand and grab the short end of the wire with the round-nose pliers. Begin to turn your wrist to form a round loop. Release the wire and reposition your wrist and round-nose pliers as needed.

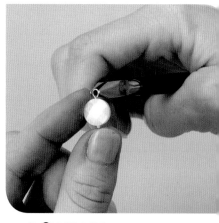

5. CLOSE GAPS
With the chain-nose pliers, carefully close up any gaps in the loop. Apply gentle pressure to avoid crushing the loop.

WIRE-WRAPPED LOOPED DANGLE

As your skills grow, I recommend this technique over the Simple Looped Dangle (page 20) as it provides a more polished look as well as durability to your jewelry.

At step 3, you will often need to insert a link of chain or other wire wrap into the loop before it's closed. In order to prevent damaging that loop, you might wish to hold the round-nose pliers inside the loop (shown below), instead of across the loop.

1. ADD BEADS
Slide the bead(s) onto a headpin.

2. BEND WIRE
With the round-nose pliers, bend the headpin wire to 90 degrees, about 1/16" (2mm) above the top of the bead.

3. WRAP WIRE
Position the round-nose pliers so they sit directly in the corner of the angle made in step 2. With your fingers, press the tail of the wire around the round jaw of the round-nose pliers 1 time. (Insert the end of a chain, an earring hook or another looped wire before the loop is closed.)

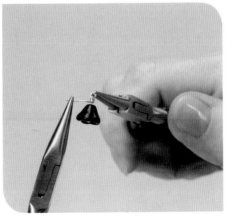

4. WRAP WIRE
Grab the short tail end of the wire with the chain-nose pliers and wrap it around the base of the loop 2 or 3 times to secure. Release the wire and reposition your wrist and chain-nose pliers as needed.

5. CUT EXCESS WIRE AND FINISH
Cut the excess wire with the side cutters. Press down any sharp edges with the chain-nose pliers.

WIRE WRAPPING A TOP-DRILLED BEAD

Most beads are drilled top-to-bottom. However, there are many gorgeous beads that are top-drilled, which means the hole is drilled horizontally from side-to-side at the tip of the bead. This is often the case with teardrop-shaped or briolette beads.

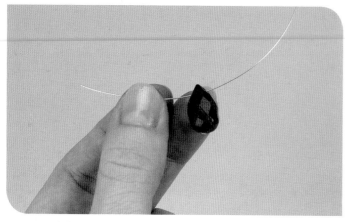

1. Cut and insert wire
Cut approximately 3" (8cm) of 26-gauge, half-hard wire. Insert the wire through the top-drilled bead.

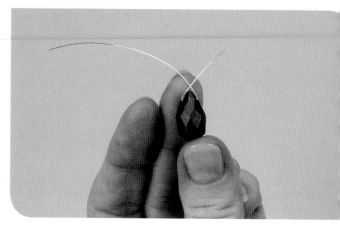

2. Fold wire
With about 1" (3cm) of the wire through the hole, fold it over the side of the bead and then fold the longer end over so that they are crossing.

3. Bend wire
Directly above the center point of the bead, add a vertical bend to the long end of the wire with the chain-nose pliers, so the wire is now pointing straight up.

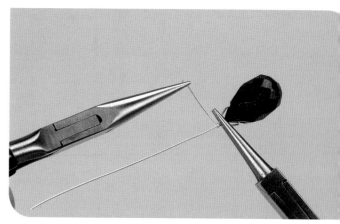

4. Wrap wires
With the round-nose pliers, hold both sides of the triangle steady. With the chain-nose pliers, take the shorter end of the wire and wrap it around the long wire 2 or 3 times as close as possible right above the triangle formed by the crossed wires.

5. CUT EXCESS WIRE
With the flush wire cutters, cut the wire as close as possible to the wrap. Press down any sharp cut edges with the chain-nose pliers.

6. COVER GAP
Leave about ¹⁄₁₆" (2mm) gap above the wrap you created in step 4. Bend the long vertical wire 90 degrees with the round-nose pliers. Wrap a loop around the end of the round-nose pliers. Then reposition the round-nose pliers to hold across the newly created loop. With the chain-nose pliers in your other hand, wrap the end of the wire to cover ¹⁄₁₆" (2mm) gap.

WIRE WRAPPING A TOP-DRILLED BEAD WITH AN ACCENT BEAD

I find this option slightly easier and neater for the beginner. With 3"–3½" (8cm–9cm) of wire, follow steps 1–5 from Wire Wrapping a Top-Drilled Bead (page 22), then start here with step 1.

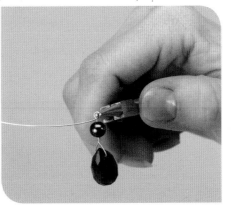

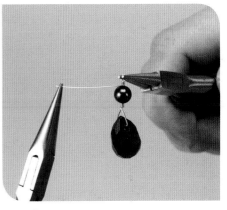

1. ADD BEAD
Thread the accent bead onto the wire.

2. CREATE A LOOP
Leave a small gap [¹⁄₁₆" (2mm)] directly above the bead, just enough to wrap the wire around 2 or 3 times. Bend the wire 90 degrees. Wrap the wire around the top of the round-nose pliers.

3. CLOSE THE LOOP
To close the loop, grab the end of the wire with the chain-nose pliers and wrap around the base 2 or 3 times to secure. Flush cut the wire, and press down the sharp cut end with the chain-nose pliers.

CREATING A WIRE SPIRAL

Several of the earrings featured in this book use a wire spiral design, either on the main earring component or on the earring hook. Spiraling the wire provides a fun, artisan look to your designs. But, take it slow—this technique takes some practice. Use a base metal wire until you get the hang of it. The gauge and length of the wire will depend on its use. I provide suggestions in the each of the instances where spirals are used in this book.

1. START SPIRAL
Start with 5" (13cm) of straightened, half-hard 20- or 22-gauge wire. With the round-nose pliers, turn 1 end of the wire into a round "p" shape. Tuck in the end so that it sits against the wire or even slightly tucked into the circle.

2. PRESS THE WIRE
With the flat-nose pliers, hold the small p-loop from step 1. With your other hand, hold your thumb against the wire, so that it presses the wire against the loop you made in step 1.

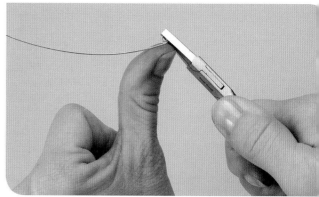

3. TURN YOUR WRIST
Holding the spiral steady in your hand, turn the flat-nose pliers a quarter turn. Release the flat-nose pliers, and reposition them at the end of the spiral. Repeat until the spiral is the size you desire.

*See **Ocean Treasure** (page 76) and **Coral Spiral** (page 60) for projects using this technique.*

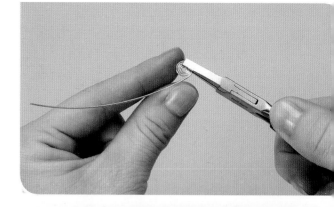

CREATING A COIL WRAP

A few of the projects use a coil wrap to act as a "stopper" to keep beads from falling off the earring hooks or to wrap beads onto metal components. Use plated wire until you get the hang of this technique!

1. CUT WIRE

Cut about 5"-6" (13cm-15cm) of 26- or 28-gauge wire.

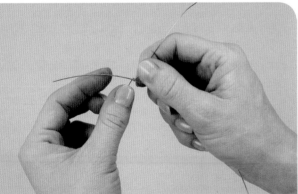

2. BEGIN COIL

About 1" (3cm) from the end of the wire, start to wrap the wire around the earring hook or hoop that needs the "stopper." Wrap the wire 2 or 3 times and push the coils tightly together using the chain-nose pliers to collapse the space in between the wraps, if necessary.

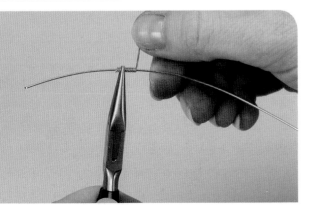

3. WRAP IN OPPOSITE DIRECTION

Take the long end of the wire and wrap it in the opposite direction, carefully wrapping to about $\frac{1}{4}$" (6mm), more or less to suit your aesthetic taste.

Use chain-nose pliers to hold the coils steady while you wrap the wire into a coil with your other hand.

CREATING YOUR OWN EARRING HOOKS

While earring hooks can be easily purchased at any craft or jewelry supply store, handmade hooks can really set a pair of earrings apart from standard store-bought earrings. Artistic hooks are surprisingly simple, fun and inexpensive to make. When deciding on earring hooks, consider the shapes of the beads you are working with.

I prefer to use 20- or 21-gauge sterling silver or gold-filled wire for my earring hook designs. There are a few tools that will be helpful when making earring hooks (see the Earring Hook Tool Kit on pages 12–13). You can make hooks in a variety of shapes and sizes. See Simple Brushed Silver (page 34) for an example of a design featuring round hooks, Modern Geometry (page 46) for elongated hooks and Sunshine Hoops (page 38) for almond-shaped hooks.

ROUND EARRING HOOKS

These big, round earring hooks have a modern, bold style that is decidedly artistic. They're perfect to pair with round focal beads.

> To stiffen the earring hooks, hammer the finished design with your chasing hammer or hard plastic mallet. This will work-harden the wire to help it retain its shape.

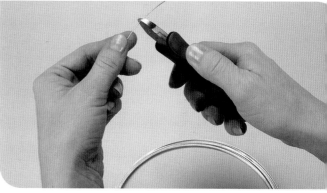

1. CUT WIRES
Cut 2 pieces of 20- or 21-gauge wire each about 3"–3½" (8cm–9cm) long, depending on the desired diameter. (If needed, straighten wire before cutting.)

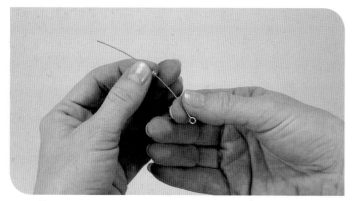

2. CREATE LOOP AND DECORATE
At the end of the wire, create a simple or wire-wrapped loop [see Creating a Wire Loop: Simple Loop (page 16)]. If desired, you can add a 2mm or 3mm spacer, crystal or other small bead at the base to decorate the hooks.

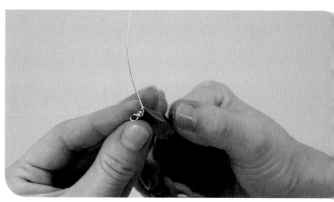

3. BEND WIRE
Using the chain-nose pliers, bend the wire 90 degrees toward the front of the hook, taking care not to crush the accent bead, if applicable.

4. WRAP TO CREATE HOOK

Grasp the loop end with your fore-finger and thumb and press it firmly around the mandrel. Wrap the wire all the way around the mandrel until it reaches past the loop. Release the wire.

5. CUT OFF EXCESS WIRE

Use the flush cutters to snip any excess wire that reaches past the loop.

6. BEND AND FILE WIRE

Bend the last ¼" (6mm) of the wire end back slightly and file to smooth down any sharp ends.

You can use the end of a ring mandrel, the smooth barrel of a marker, or just about any round and smooth object to shape an earring hook. The finished loop may be larger than the object you use after the wire is released. I find that size 3 on a ring mandrel makes a nicely sized loop for the round hooks.

EARRING HOOK ASSEMBLY

Whether you make your hooks or buy them, adding your handmade bead dangles is an easy two-step process.

1. OPEN LOOP

To open the loop on an earring hook, gently twist the loop sideways with your chain-nose pliers.

2. ADD DANGLE AND CLOSE LOOP

Slide the looped bead dangle onto the open loop on the earring hook. Gently twist the loop sideways back into its original closed position. **27**

SIMPLE FRENCH HOOKS

These classic, graceful earring hooks are a cinch to make! The advantage of this simple loop style is that you can open the loop and attach it after the earring design is completed.

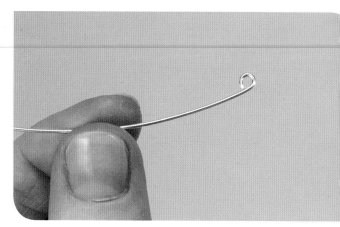

1. CUT WIRE
Cut 2¼"–3½" (6cm–9cm) wire, depending on the curve radius and the length of the tail that you desire.

2. CREATE SMALL LOOP
Grab the end of the wire with round-nose pliers and wrap 1 full turn of the wrist, making a "p" shape.

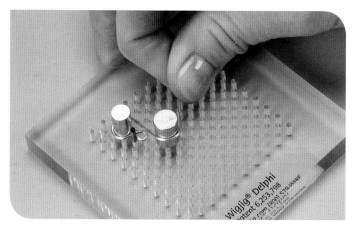

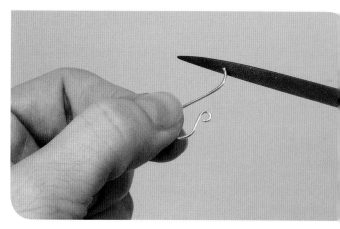

3. CONTINUE SHAPING WIRE
In the opposite direction of this small loop, press the wire against the barrel of a smooth pen (page 29, step 3), or use a wire jig. (See page 13 for a sample wire-jig layout.) When using a pen, slightly bend up the last ¼" (6mm) of the tail with the chain-nose pliers, if desired.

4. FILE
File in 1 direction with a needle file to smooth down any rough edges. If desired, flatten the tail of the hook with a chasing hammer [see Hammering (page 15)]. If you prefer the rounded shape of the wire, use the hard plastic mallet instead to work-harden the wire.

FRENCH HOOKS WITH SPIRAL

This design accent makes the earring hooks part of the complete design.

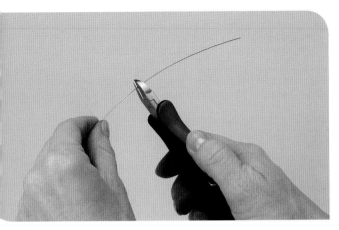

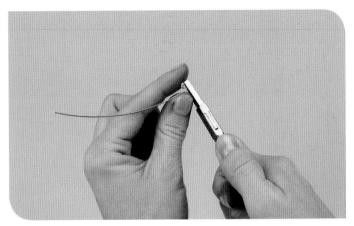

1. CUT WIRE

Straighten the 20- or 21-gauge wire with nylon-jaw pliers before cutting. Cut a length of about 3½" (9cm) of wire.

2. CREATE SPIRAL

Create a wire spiral at the end of the wire [see Creating a Wire Spiral (page 24)]. Start with a center hole that is large enough to insert the wire loop that connects the body of the earring design. Wrap around about 2 times.

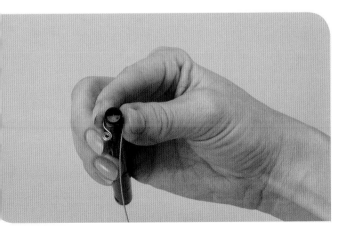

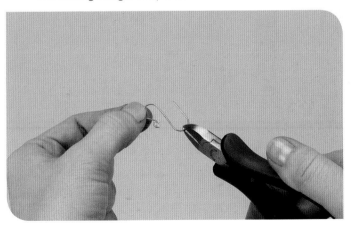

3. SHAPE CURVE

Hold the spiral tangent to a thick marker or highlighter (shown) and wrap the wire around, or use a wire jig. (See step 3 photo on page 28.) Bend up the last ¼" (6mm) of the tail slightly with the chain-nose pliers.

4. CUT EXCESS WIRE AND FILE

Cut wire tail to desired length and file the end of the wire to smooth any rough edges [see Filing (page 15)].

*See **Sun and Sea Swing** (page 62) or **Coral Spiral** (page 60) for projects that feature French hooks with spirals.*

SIMPLE WIRE HOOPS

These are super simple to make, and with just a little bit of wire, you can be sure to have hoops of any size you desire! I recommend using half-hard sterling silver or gold-filled wire so the hoops retain their shape better.

GENERAL SIZES OF WIRE

For 1" (3cm) hoops use 4" (10cm) of wire
For 1¼" (3cm) hoops use 5" (13cm) of wire
For 1½" (4cm) hoops use 5½" (14cm) of wire

In this earring style, part of the wire of the hoop goes directly through the ear. Because of this, it's important to leave at least ½" (1cm) at the front of the earring to accommodate the thickness of the earlobe.

1. STRAIGHTEN AND CUT WIRE

Before cutting the 20- or 21-gauge wire, run the nylon-jaw pliers over it a few times to straighten it. Cut 2 pieces of the wire, using the chart at left to determine the length.

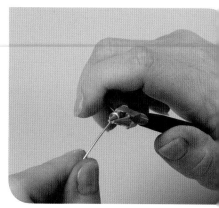

2. CREATE LOOP

At the end of the wire, create a simple or wire-wrapped loop [see Creating a Wire Loop (pages 16–17)].

3. FORM CIRCLE

Wrap the wire around the base of a ring mandrel or a 1" (3cm) object—or to the desired size. Don't worry about wrapping around more than once. The wire will spring into a circle when released. If you plan to thread beads on the hoop, do that now.

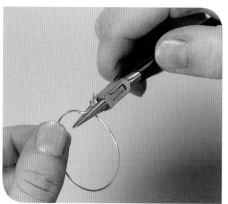

4. CREATE HOOK FOR HOOP

At the point where the end of the wire crosses past the loop, use the round-nose pliers to bend the wire up 90 degrees to create a smooth curved bend.

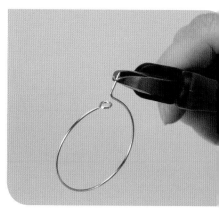

5. CUT TAIL AND FINISH

Cut the tail about ¼" (6mm) long. File it smooth.

*See **Mirror, Mirror Hoops** (page 96) for a project using handcrafted hoops.*

HANGING WIRE HOOPS

These are hoops that require earring hooks to be added to them. This design allows you to decorate the entire hoop, as you don't need to leave space for the wire to go through the ear.

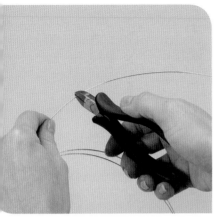

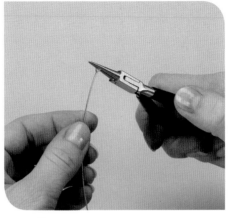

1. STRAIGHTEN AND CUT WIRE

Before cutting the 20- or 21-gauge wire, run the nylon-jaw pliers over it a few times to straighten it. Cut 2 pieces of wire approximately 7" (18cm) long.

2. CREATE LOOP

At the end of the wire, create a simple or wire-wrapped loop [see Creating a Wire Loop (pages 16–17)]. Make sure the loop is perpendicular to the natural curve of the wire.

3. ADD BEND

Leave about ⅛" (3mm) gap below the loop, and create a 90-degree bend perpendicular to the loop you made in step 2.

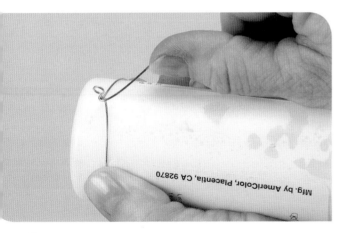

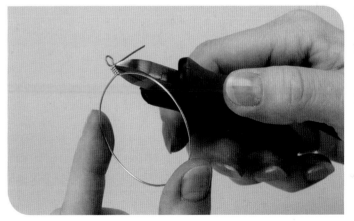

4. SHAPE HOOP AND WRAP WIRE

Wrap the wire around a mandrel of your desired hoop size [approximately 1"– 1½" (3cm–4cm)]. At the point where the tail crosses the bend you created in step 3, wrap the tail around the ⅛" (3mm) gap 3 or 4 times.

5. CUT WIRE

Cut the excess wire and press down any sharp edges with your chain-nose pliers.

everyday favorites

There are a few earring designs in my collection that I could wear day after day. They transition perfectly from a business meeting to dinner with friends after work. They're the earrings I pack in my weekend-getaway bag because I know they'll go with anything. Here are a few designs that will surely earn an honorable place in your jewelry box.

SimpleBrushedSilver

Earring hooks can be one of the most important design elements of your earrings. When deciding on earring hooks, consider the shape of the beads you're working with. The round earring hooks in this design echo the coin-shaped beads to make a perfect match.

30 min.

Length: 1" (3cm)

TECHNIQUES

Creating your own Earring Hooks:
Round Hooks (page 26)
Creating a Looped Dangle:
Simple Looped Dangle (page 20)
Creating a Wire Loop:
Simple Loop (page 16)

TOOLS

Basic Tool Kit
Earring Hook Tool Kit

MATERIALS

4 3mm silver spacer beads
2 10mm brushed silver beads
2 headpins
2 round earring hooks

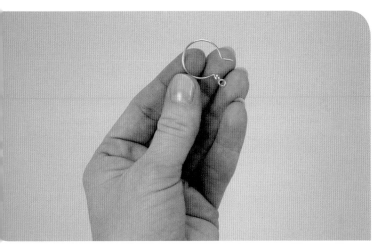

1. CREATE HOOKS

Create 2 sterling silver, round earring hooks using 2 3mm silver spacer beads as accents, if desired.

> Depending on your focal bead, you may wish to refer to wire wrapping a top-drilled bead (page 22).

2. CREATE DANGLE

Slide the 10mm brushed-silver bead on a headpin followed by a 3mm round spacer bead. Create a simple loop on the top of the bead.

> If the hole on the bead is too large to rest on the end of the headpin, place a small spacer bead on the end to block the hole.

3. INSERT HOOK

Gently open the top loop and insert the earring hook. Close the loop. Repeat for the other earring.

SimpleElegance

These earrings are so fast and easy to make, you'll want them in every color! Be creative...changing the colors or materials transforms the entire mood of the earrings.

15 min.

Length: 1" (3cm)

TECHNIQUES

Creating a Looped Dangle:
Wire-Wrapped Looped Dangle (page 21)
Creating a Looped Bead:
Wire-Wrapped Looped Bead (page 19)

TOOLS

Basic Tool Kit

MATERIALS

2 8mm pacific opal Swarovski
crystal rondelle beads
2 4mm indicolite Swarovski
crystal bicone beads
4 4mm silver daisy spacer beads
2 7mm fancy soldered-closed jump rings
2 headpins
5" (13cm) 24- or 26-gauge,
half-hard sterling silver wire
2 earring hooks

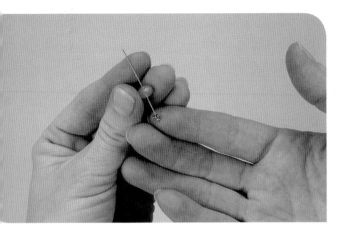

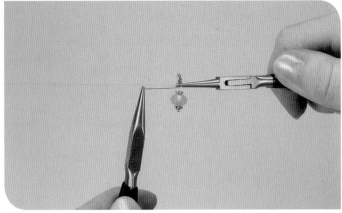

1. SLIDE ON BEADS AND SPACERS

Start by sliding onto a headpin in order: 1 daisy spacer, 1 8mm crystal rondelle and 1 daisy spacer.

2. ADD AND SECURE JUMP RING

Begin to create an open loop. Insert the decorative jump ring into the loop and then close it securely with 2 or 3 wire wraps. Put this piece aside.

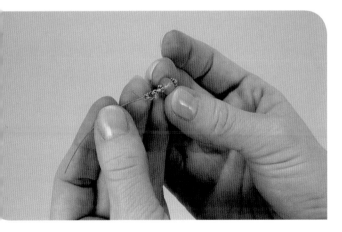

3. CREATE LOOP

With 2½" (6cm) of wire, create an open loop and add the jump ring with the connected rondelle. Close the loop with 2 or 3 wraps.

*See **The Essential Black Earrings** (page 134) for another example of using a decorative metal connector between two beads.*

4. ADD CRYSTAL AND FINISH

On the tail of the wire, slide on 1 4mm bicone crystal. Create a wire-wrapped loop at the top of the bicone and close it securely with 2 or 3 wraps. Connect the earring hook into the top loop and repeat for the other earring.

Sunshine Hoops

There's something very gratifying about having a hand in the redefinition of a simple piece of wire into an artistically sculpted jewelry component. These unusual almond-shaped earring wires give this design a modern, graceful contour. This style can spotlight a single stunning briolette, or host a collection of lovely little beads.

30 min.

Length: 2" (5cm)

TECHNIQUES

Creating a Wire Loop: Wire-Wrapped Loop (page 17)
Creating Your Own Earring Hooks: Simple Wire Hoops (page 30)
Wire Wrapping a Top-Drilled Bead (page 22)
Filing (page 15)
Hammering (page 15)

TOOLS

Basic Tool Kit
Earring Hook Tool Kit

MATERIALS

2 10 x 10mm chalcedony faceted briolettes
10" (25cm) 20- or 21-gauge, half-hard, gold-filled wire
6" (15cm) 24- or 26-gauge, half-hard, gold-filled wire

1. CUT WIRE AND MAKE LOOP

Cut 2 lengths of 20- or 21-gauge wire, 5" (13cm) each. At the end of each wire, make a wire-wrapped loop.

2. Create curve and cut overlap

To give the wire its distinctive curved shape, press the looped end of the wire against the base of a ring mandrel [or other 1" (3cm) round sturdy object] and begin to wrap it fully around. With the flush cutters, cut the wire at the point where the ends of the wire overlap. Release the wire from around the mandrel.

3. Form almond shape

Position the chain-nose pliers at the halfway mark at the top of the hoop, and gently turn your wrist to create a "fish" shape. Release the wire, and gently pull apart, forming a smooth almond shape. Trim off ¼" (6mm) from the tail. Repeat these instructions with the other 5" (13cm) of wire. Trim the 2 earring hooks to be the same size and curve. File the ends of the hooks (in 1 direction only) with a small metal file to remove any sharp edges.

4. Align loop

With the chain-nose pliers, bend the wire at the end of the earring hook with the closed loop so that the loop will hang directly down.

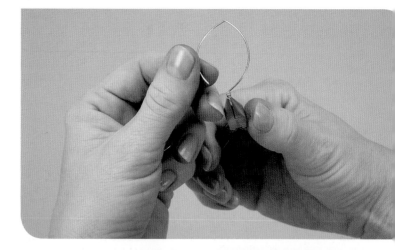

5. Hammer hook

Carefully hammer the earring hook with the hard plastic mallet on the steel block. This will help to work-harden the wire and retain its almond shape. Alternatively, you can use the chasing hammer if you prefer a flattened look.

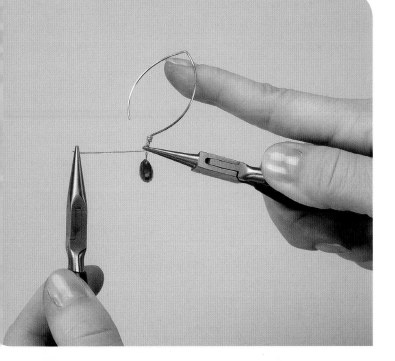

6. Wrap bead

With 3" (8cm) of 24- or 26-gauge wire, wrap the briolette to the bottom loop on the earring hook. Repeat for the other earring.

Make sure that the smaller wire will fit through the beads of your choice.

Smoky Quartz Briolette

This long, classic style is professional, yet elegant and sophisticated. The earthy color palette will go with just about everything, day to night and work to play. Experiment with your favorite colors! This adaptable pattern can easily be converted to shades of pink for spring, or black and silver for a formal occasion.

30 min.

Length: 2" (5cm)

TECHNIQUES

Creating a Wire Loop:
Wire-Wrapped Loop (page 17)
Wire Wrapping a Top-Drilled Bead
with an Accent Bead (page 23)

TOOLS

Basic Tool Kit

MATERIALS

2 10 x 10mm smoky quartz faceted briolettes
4 5–6mm bronze freshwater pearls
2 6mm smoky quartz
Swarovski crystal bicone beads
2 6mm garnet faceted beads
18" (46m) 26-gauge, half-hard, gold-filled wire
2 earring hooks

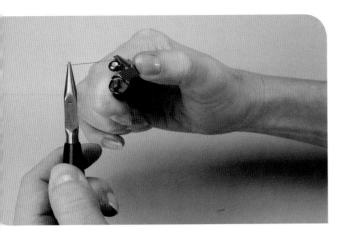

1. WRAP BEAD AND ADD PEARL

With 3" (8cm) of wire, wrap the briolette and add 1 of
the freshwater pearls on top. Put this piece aside.

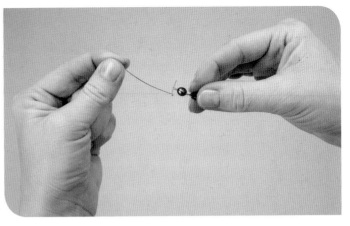

2. CREATE OPEN LOOP AND ADD BEADS

Take 2" (5cm) of wire and create an open loop. Slide the
wrapped pearl and briolette piece you made in step 1
onto this open loop. Close the loop securely with 2 or 3
wraps of wire.

3. ADD BEAD

Slide the 6mm bicone crystal onto the tail of the wire.
Above the crystal, create a closed wire-wrapped loop
as you did in step 2.

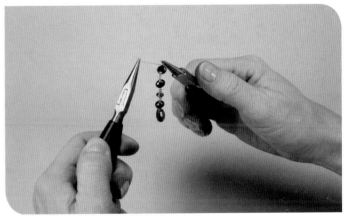

4. ADD REMAINING BEADS AND FINISH

Repeat steps 2 and 3 for the bronze pearl, and again for
the garnet, adding each to the closed loop of the previous
bead. Attach the earring hook to the last loop on top of
the garnet and repeat for the other earring.

Working9to5

Look your best while punching the time clock! Being professional and work-appropriate doesn't mean you have to sacrifice your sense of style. Work with colors that are subtle or muted and materials that are classic, such as crystal, pearls and semiprecious stones. The designs in this section will demonstrate that you can look sharp, polished and refined without losing your panache.

ModernGeometry

You will never believe that these classically modern earrings can be
made so easily and inexpensively.

30 min.

Length: 2" (5cm)

TECHNIQUES

Creating a Wire Loop:
Wire-Wrapped Loop (page 17)
Filing (page 15)

TOOLS

Basic Tool Kit
Earring Hook Tool Kit

MATERIALS

2 8mm carnelian faceted
round beads
12" (31cm) 20- or 21-gauge,
half-hard, gold-filled wire

**Be sure the wire will fit through
the holes in your focal beads.**

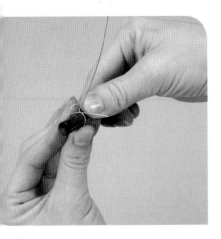

1. Cut wires and shape wires

Cut 2 lengths of the wire, 6" (15cm) each. About 1½" (4cm) from the end of the wire, press the wire around a smooth-barreled writing pen [³⁄₈" (1cm)]. Cross the ends of the wire around it. At the junction of the 2 wires, bend the long wire up 90 degrees with the chain-nose pliers.

2. Wrap tail around base

While holding the circle shape steady against the pen, wrap the shorter tail of the wire around the base 2 or 3 times with your fingers or the chain-nose pliers. Cut excess wire and press down sharp edges.

3. Add bead

If needed, straighten the wire again. Slide 1 carnelian bead to rest on top of the circle loop.

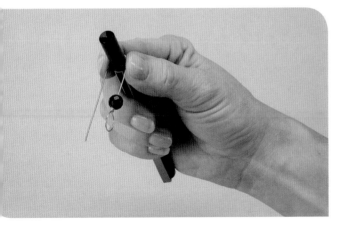

4. Shape earring

Hold a pen at the desired height of the earring. [I recommend about 1½" (4cm).] Wrap the wire around the pen, forming an elongated "U" shape perpendicular to the circle.

5. Cut tail and finish

Cut the back tail of the earring hook to the desired length. In this example, the long tail gives this earring a modern, artisan look. Bend the last ¼" (6mm) of the wire up slightly and file to smooth away any rough edges. Repeat for the other earring.

Butterscotch**Cluster**

Classic matte gold and subtle shades of brown blend to create a polished, confident palette in these sophisticated earrings. Always-appropriate pearls and timeless crystals are clustered along the chain for a plentiful arrangement of textures and colors.

60 min.

Length: 1½" (4cm)

TECHNIQUES

Creating a Looped Dangle (pages 20–21)

Creating a Looped Bead:
Wire-Wrapped Looped Bead (page 19)

Wire Wrapping a Top-Drilled Bead (page 22)

TOOLS

Basic Tool Kit

MATERIALS

2 7 x 10mm gold brushed metal briolettes

8 3–4mm copper and bronze freshwater pearls

6 4mm smoked topaz Swarovski crystal bicone beads

4 4mm crystal copper Swarovski crystal bicone beads

2 segments of chain, 5 links each

16 headpins

12" (31cm) 26-gauge gold-plated wire

2 earring hooks

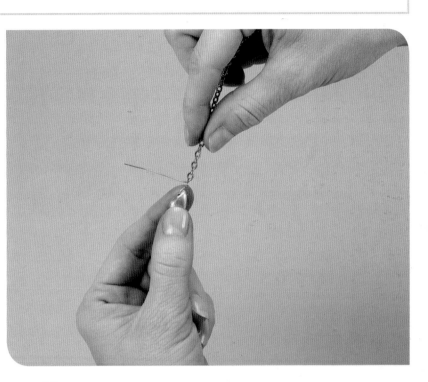

1. WRAP BEAD AND ADD CHAIN

With 3" (8cm) of wire, wrap the gold briolette. Before closing the top loop of the briolette wrap, add the first link of the gold chain. Finish closing the loop with 2 or 3 wire wraps.

To create the full look in these cluster earrings, select a chain that has links large enough to accommodate 2 headpins. If possible, keep the chain uncut, as it is easier to work with if the chain is at least a few inches (centimeters) long.

2. Create loop and add chain

Cut 2½" (6cm) of wire and begin to create an open loop. Slide the fifth link of the chain into the open loop, and then close it securely with 2 or 3 wraps. Cut off the excess chain.

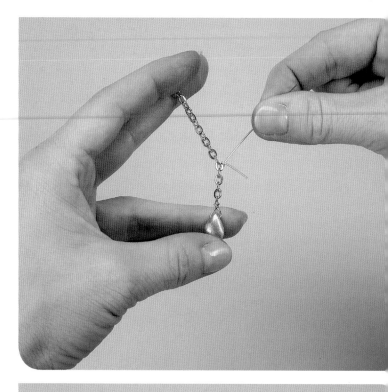

3. Add bead

Slide a smoked topaz crystal onto the remaining wire tail and make the top loop. Add the earring hook.

4. ADD DANGLES

Create a simple loop or wire-wrapped dangle. The briolette is already attached to the first link. Leave the second link empty. Add 1 freshwater pearl and 1 smoked topaz crystal to the third link. Add 1 freshwater pearl and 1 crystal copper crystal to the fourth link. Add 1 freshwater pearl and 1 smoked topaz crystal to the fifth link.

5. ADD MORE DANGLES

To retain the full clustered appearance, add 2 more bead dangles (1 freshwater pearl and 1 crystal copper crystal) to the wrapped loop located at the base of the top accent bead (smoked topaz crystal). Repeat for the other earring.

This is such an adaptable design—you can drop the cluster on the chain for an elegant variation or elongate the cluster along the chain for a vine look as shown in *Pretty In Pink Cluster* (page 122). You can even try reversing the direction of the cluster for another fun variation, as in the *City Lights Crystal* (page 147).

AntiquedCopperLantern

There's a glow and warmth from the shimmering crystal that dangles below the chain that reminds me of those romantic, flickering antique gas lamps. Experiment with different lengths, chain designs, beads and colors to make it perfect for you!

15 min.

Length: 2½" (6cm)

TECHNIQUES

Creating a Looped Bead (pages 18–19)
Creating a Looped Dangle (pages 20–21)

TOOLS

Basic Tool Kit

MATERIALS

2 12mm crystal copper
Swarovski rondelle beads

2 6mm Czech fire-polished
bronze beads

4 4mm daisy spacer
antiqued copper beads

8 2mm round spacer
antiqued copper beads

3" (8cm) antiqued copper
rolo chain (length to suit)

2 antique copper headpins

5" (13cm) 24- or 26- gauge
antiqued copper wire

2 earring hooks

If you have trouble finding antiqued copper wire, you can clip off the heads of long headpins and use the remaining wire.

1. CUT CHAIN

Cut 2 identical lengths of chain, based on your desired length of earrings. In this example, each chain is about 1½" (4cm) long (12 links).

2. ADD SPACERS AND BEADS

Slide 1 round spacer, 1 daisy spacer, 1 12mm crystal rondelle, 1 daisy spacer and 1 round spacer onto a headpin.

3. CREATE LOOP AND ADD CHAIN

Create a simple loop or wire-wrapped dangle. If you're using the wire-wrapped method, be sure to add the cut chain into the top loop of the dangle before closing the loop.

4. ADD A LOOPED BEAD TO TOP AND FINISH

With about 2½" (6cm) of wire, create a simple loop at 1 end. Thread on a round spacer, a 6mm fire polished bead, and another spacer. Create a loop on the top of the bead. If you are using the wire-wrapped method, add the chain to the bottom loop before wrapping the wire loops closed. For the simple loop method, reopen the loop and insert the chain (shown). Add the earring hook to the top loop. Repeat for the other earring.

AroundtheWorld

The cool, watery kyanite, earthy rusty-red carnelian and warm, sunny tone of the gold wire harmonize to create a sophisticated metaphor for these artistic, one-of-a-kind earrings. Successful design, in any medium, creates a synergetic relationship between all the incorporated materials.

60 min.

Length: 1¼" (3cm)

TECHNIQUES

Creating a Looped Dangle (pages 20–21)
Wire Wrapping a Top-Drilled Bead (page 22)

TOOLS

Basic Tool Kit

MATERIALS

20 3mm carnelian faceted beads
2 10 x 15mm kyanite smooth ovals (Select beads with holes large enough for 2 26-gauge wires to pass through.)
20 headpins
24" (61cm) 26-gauge gold-plated wire
2 earring hooks

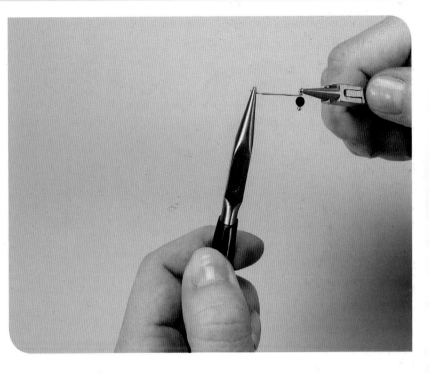

1. CREATE DANGLES
Using the simple-looped or wire-wrapped technique, create 20 dangles by sliding each of the carnelian beads onto a headpin. Set these aside.

2. Thread beads and dangles

With a 12" (31cm) piece of wire, thread the kyanite bead to the 3" (8cm) mark, and then curve the long end of the wire around the bottom of the focal bead. Thread 10 of the carnelian dangles onto the long curved wire.

Although the oval focal bead is not top-drilled, we will be using the same technique in order to create the wrapped wire effect on the top of this earring.

3. Thread wire back through bead

Carefully reinsert the long end of the wire back through the hole in the kyanite (going the opposite direction as the first insertion). Bend up both wires toward the top of the focal bead.

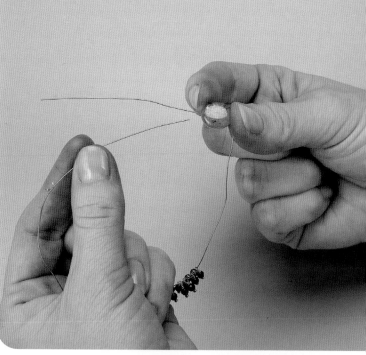

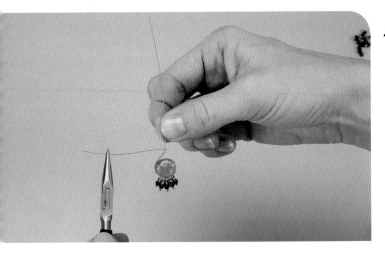

4. Wrap bead

Cross the wires over each other on the top of the kyanite bead, leaving a small triangle of space. Bend the long wire so that it's pointed straight up. Wrap the shorter wire 2 or 3 times around the bent wire to secure. Flush cut and press down sharp edges.

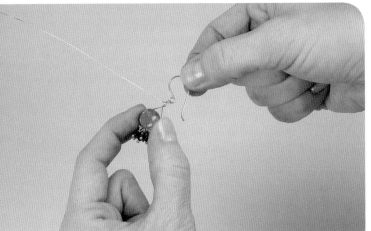

5. Slide ear wire onto loop

Start to create an open loop perpendicular to the direction of the loop on the ear wire. Slide the ear wire onto the open loop and then close the loop securely with 2 or 3 wraps.

6. Finish wrap

Continue wrapping back down the triangle space, covering it with the remaining long end of the wire. You can give the earrings a more formal look by being cautious not to overlap the wires or leave gaps, or you can wildly wrap for a more organic, playful look. Repeat for the other earring.

weekendescape

Countdown to Friday! Finally a chance to unwind and recharge. Relaxing afternoons spent with family and friends, sipping lemonade by the pool and tending the BBQ. Trade in your work clothes for your worn-in jeans and a comfy T-shirt. It's time to be bright and bold, carefree and full of vitality. The designs in this section are lively, lighthearted and playful. Have fun!

CoralSpiral

The bright, primary color and simple geometry of these red coral coin-shaped beads are unfussy and easy-going. The silver spiral on this design echoes the shape of the bead and gives this piece a playful and handcrafted artisan quality. Flat-sided focal beads work best in this design, but don't feel limited to just circles!

60 min.

Length: 1" (3cm)

TECHNIQUES

Creating a Wire Spiral (page 24)

Creating a Looped Dangle (pages 20–21)

TOOLS

Basic Tool Kit

Earring Hook Tool Kit

MATERIALS

2 15mm coral coin-shaped beads (flat)

2 6mm decorative silver beads

4 2 x 3mm silver saucer spacer beads

10" (25cm) 22-gauge
half-hard sterling silver wire

2 earring hooks

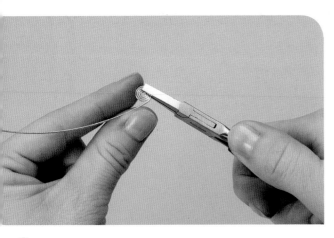

1. CREATE WIRE SPIRAL

Cut about 5" (13cm) of 22-gauge sterling silver wire. Create a wire spiral approximately 1/4"–3/8" (6mm–1cm) in diameter.

2. BEND WIRE TO CREATE "SADDLE"

Bend the wire 90 degrees perpendicular to the spiral. Leave a gap of about 1/8" (3mm), or about half the thickness of the focal bead, and then bend the wire up 90 degrees again, forming a tight "U" shape.

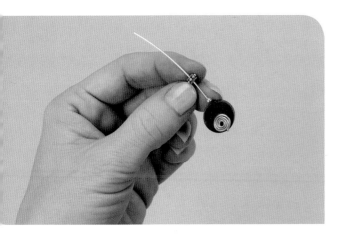

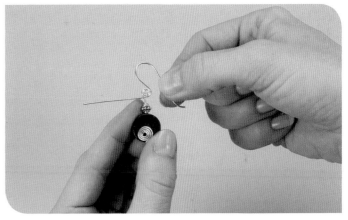

3. ADD BEADS

Slide the focal bead onto the long wire, followed by a saucer spacer, a decorative silver bead and another spacer.

4. ADD HOOK

Start to create an open loop using either the simple-looped or wire-wrapped looped dangle method, add the earring hook, and then close it securely with 2 or 3 wraps. Repeat for other earring.

Optional: Try creating some handmade spiral French earring hooks (see page 29) to match the spiral motif on the focal bead as shown here.

SunandSeaSwing

60 min.

You can almost feel the warmth from the sun's rays radiating from the gold chains in this design. The delicate swaying chains allow the faceted zircon to rock buoyantly like the waves on the ocean. The faceted orange carnelian draws subtle references to the sun in the sky.

Length: 2" (5cm)

TECHNIQUES

Creating a Looped Dangle:
Wire-Wrapped Looped Dangle (page 21)

Creating a Looped Bead:
Wire-Wrapped Looped Bead (page 19)

TOOLS

Basic Tool Kit

Earring Hook Tool Kit (optional)

MATERIALS

2 3-4mm carnelian faceted beads

12 3-4mm zircon faceted beads

18" (46cm) gold-filled chain, delicate links

5" (13cm) 26-gauge, half-hard, gold-filled wire

12 headpins

2 earring hooks

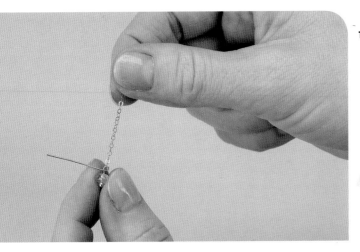

1. Cut chains and create dangles

Cut 12 pieces of chain approximately 1¼" (3cm) long (count the links of each piece if you want to make sure they're all exactly the same length). To create the dangles on the chain tassels, insert a headpin into the faceted zircon bead. Begin to make a wire-wrapped loop and insert the last link on the chain before wrapping it 2 or 3 times to close. Repeat for each piece of chain.

To ensure that the dangles won't fall off the chain, I recommend using the wire-wrapped method over the simple loop method, but feel free to use whatever method is more comfortable for you.

2. Create tassel

With about 2½" (6cm) of wire, create an open loop. Insert 6 chains into the loop before securing it closed with 2 or 3 wraps.

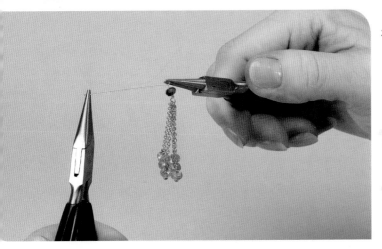

3. Add bead and top loop

Slide the faceted carnelian bead onto the tail of the wire and make a wire-wrapped loop at the top. Connect the earring hook to the top loop and repeat steps 2 and 3 to create the other earring.

Optional: Try creating some handmade spiral French earring hooks to give this design a playful feel. (See page 29.)

*See **Red Carpet Tassel** (page 136) for a variation on this design.*

BombayHoops

Experiment with colors and textures for the beads in this design; virtually any rounded bead about 3–4mm will work! This design doesn't require a separate earring hook. One end of the hoop slides directly through the ear lobe. Use a smaller mandrel for petite earrings or a larger mandrel for adventurously bold hoops!

60 min.

Length: 1¼" (3cm)
diameter hoops

TECHNIQUES

Creating your own Earring Hooks:
Simple Wire Hoops (page 30)

Creating a Coil Wrap (page 25)

TOOLS

Basic Tool Kit

1" (3cm) diameter mandrel

MATERIALS

10" (25m) 20- or 21-gauge
half-hard gold-filled wire

32" (81cm) 26- or 28-gauge
half-hard gold-filled wire

22 3mm garnet faceted round beads

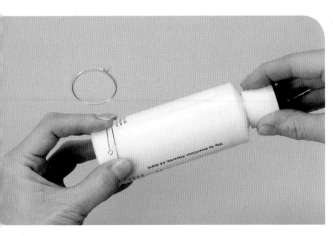

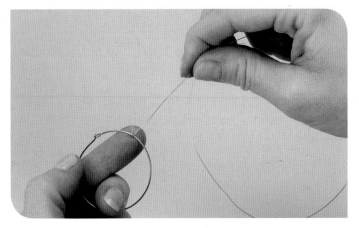

1. Cut wire and create hoops

Using the 20- or 21- gauge wire, create 2 earring hoops approximately 1¼" (3cm) in diameter. You can use just about any round object to create the diameter you want. You can also use premade hoops.

2. Make coil wrap

To wrap the beads, cut about 16" (41cm) of 26- or 28-gauge, half-hard wire [for 1¼" (3cm) diameter hoops]. With about ¾" (2cm) tail, hold the wire at about the 2 o'clock mark on the hoop, and coil the short tail of the wire up toward the top of the hoop with your fingers. Wrap around 5–6 times, then cut. Tuck the sharp end down with the chain-nose pliers. Keep the coil steady by holding it with the chain-nose pliers.

3. Add beads

Once the coil is secure on the hoop, thread 1 of the garnet beads on the free, long end of the wire. Hold the garnet in 1 hand securely on the outside ridge of the hoop. With the other hand, continue to coil the wire around the hoop in the same direction as you started. Coil around as closely as possible without overlapping or leaving gaps. If there is a gap, squeeze the coils together with your fingernails until the gap closes.

4. Cut wire and finish

Repeat step 3 with the garnet beads until it is symmetrical to the starting point on the other side. Remember to leave enough space in the front of the hoop to accommodate your ear lobe! Cut the end of the wire at the last coil, and press any sharp edges in with the chain-nose pliers. Repeat with the other hoop.

*For more hoop styles, see **Rose Garden Hoops** (page 92) and **Mirror, Mirror Hoops** (page 96).*

FireworksinAquaandMocha

Elevate the status of a plain piece of wire to this elegant and unique form with just a few bends and curves! By adjusting the length of wire on the dangles, the beads energetically dance and intermix, creating a visual mélange of color and texture. Feel free to play with color and shape!

60 min.

Length: 2" (5cm)

TECHNIQUES

Creating a Looped Dangle:
Wire-Wrapped Looped Dangle (page 21)

Creating a Wire Spiral (page 24)

Creating a Coil Wrap (page 25)

Creating Your Own Earring Hooks (page 26)

Filing (page 15)

Hammering (page 15)

TOOLS

Basic Tool Kit

Earring Hook Tool Kit

Wire Jig

MATERIALS

4 4mm smoked topaz Swarovski crystal bicone beads

6 4mm indicolite Swarovski crystal bicone beads

4 5mm light Colorado topaz Swarovski crystal bicone beads

6 4mm apatite faceted round beads

20 headpins

9" (23cm) 20- or 21-gauge, half-hard, gold-filled wire

10" (25cm) 26-gauge, half-hard, gold-filled wire

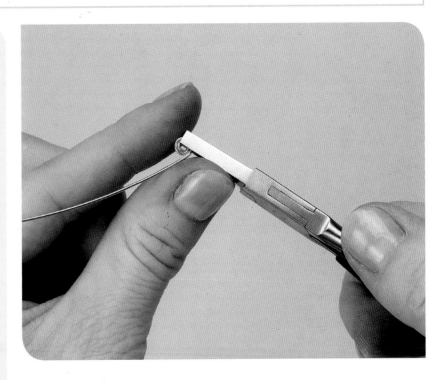

1. START SPIRAL

Straighten the thicker 20- or 21-gauge wire with the nylon-jaw pliers. Cut 2 pieces of the wire 4½" (11cm) long. Begin to create a spiral.

2. Create right angles

After 2 or 3 spirals, leave a small gap of about ⅛" (3mm) and then bend the wire to a 90-degree angle on the same side as the spiral. Leave about ½" (1cm) gap and then turn up another 90 degrees (see photo). Repeat with the other wire.

3. Shape the hook

To best match the 2 earring hooks, I recommend using a wire jig set up in the pattern shown. Otherwise, take both wires and wrap them around a highlighter or thick-barreled pen to create the desired curve of the earring hooks. Smooth the ends with the needle file.

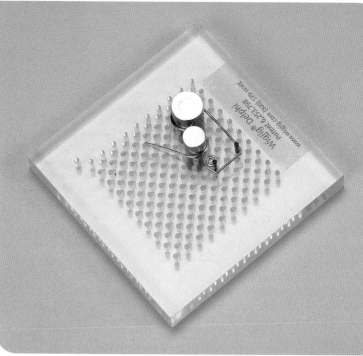

4. CREATE DANGLES

To create the firework dangles, slide each bead onto a headpin and wrap just the top part of the headpin, altering the lengths. I prefer the wire-wrapped method for making these dangles—not only for the added security, but also for the additional visual texture the wire wrap provides to the design. Slide 10 dangles onto each of the earring hooks from step 3.

5. CREATE COIL STOPPER

To keep the dangles on the hooks, you may need to create "stopper" coils on the earrings. With 5" (13cm) of 26- or 28-gauge wire, leave about 1" (3cm) tail from the end of the wire and start to wrap the wire above the 90 degree corner on the earring hook. Carefully wrap about ¼" (6mm), more or less to suit your aesthetic taste, and push the coil snugly into the corner. Repeat for the other earring.

dayat**the**beach

Ahhhh...listening to the waves lap along the sand...picking up shells along the shore...feeling the breeze across your cheeks. Don't you wish every day could be a day at the beach, far away from the stress of the workweek and routine of daily life? Find some lovely beads in tranquil, calming shades of the ocean and journey to that place, if even for just a moment.

SeaGlass

So simple, so soothing—these recycled glass earrings feature beads that seem to be smoothed by the years of marriage between the lapping waves and the sand on the beach. This is a perfect design for beginners and experts alike—it's just 1-2-3. It's as easy as a day at the beach.

15 min.

Length: ³/₄" (2cm)

TECHNIQUES

Creating a Looped Dangle:
Simple Looped Dangle (page 20)

Creating a Wire Loop:
Simple Loop (page 16)

TOOLS

Basic Tool Kit

MATERIALS

2 8 x 10mm recycled glass beads

2 6mm silver round beads

6 2 x 3mm silver saucer spacers

2 headpins

2 earring hooks

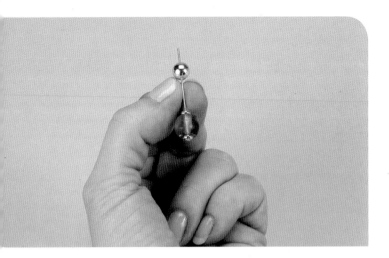

1. ADD BEADS
Slide a silver spacer, recycled glass bead, second spacer, 6mm silver round bead and third spacer onto a long headpin.

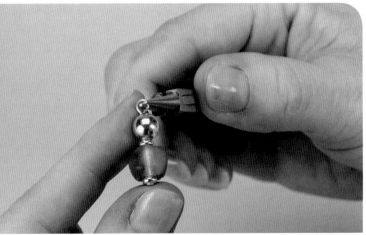

2. CREATE SIMPLE LOOP
Create a simple loop on the top of the last bead.

These instructions use the simple looped technique to make the bead dangle, but feel free to use the wire-wrapped technique (page 21) for a more secure connection between the dangle and the earring hook.

3. ADD EARRING HOOK
Gently open the top loop and insert the earring hook. Repeat for the other earring—simple as that!

CaribbeanCollage

These earrings remind me of all the shells, stones and other little treasures I collected on the beach shore as a child. The mellow colors of the freshwater pearls and mother-of-pearl beads are intermixed with sparkling crystals that hint of the ocean. Use extra beads left over from other projects to create a medley of texture and colors!

30 min.

Length: 1½" (4cm)

TECHNIQUES

Creating a Looped Dangle:
Simple Looped Dangle (page 20)

Creating a Looped Bead (page 18)

TOOLS

Basic Tool Kit

MATERIALS

2 10-15mm silver circle hoops

2 5 x 8mm keishi (or cornflake) pearls

4 4mm white rice freshwater pearls

2 10mm recycled glass beads

4 2 x 3mm silver saucer spacer beads
(if hole is large on bead above)

2 10mm mother-of-pearl coin-shaped beads

2 6mm erinite Swarovski crystal bicone beads

2 4 x 7mm pale aqua faceted rondelle beads

4 4mm silver daisy spacer beads

4" (10cm) 26-gauge, half-hard,
sterling silver wire

12 headpins

2 earring hooks

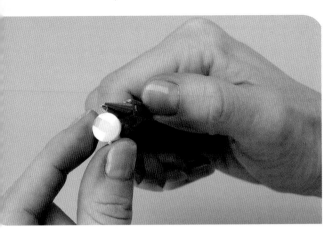

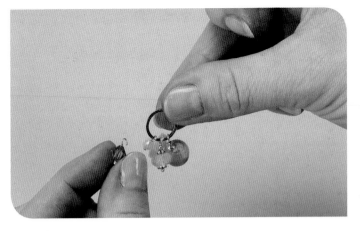

1. CREATE DANGLES

To create the bead dangles, slide each bead onto a head-pin and create a simple loop on the top. Leave the loop open for now. To vary the visual texture, match some of the larger beads with accents of silver daisy spacers or smooth silver spacers.

2. ATTACH DANGLES

Connect each of the bead dangles from step 1 onto the silver circle and close the loops. Set this piece aside.

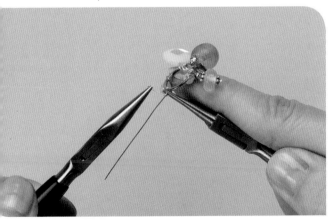

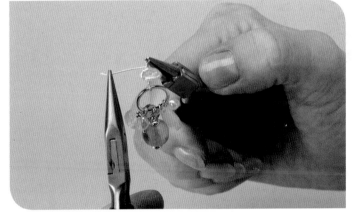

3. ADD LOOP

With 2" (5cm) of wire, begin to create an open loop and insert the silver circle with the dangles. Close the loop securely with 2 or 3 wraps.

4. ADD PEARL AND FINISH

On the tail of the wire, slide on 1 keishi pearl. Create a wire-wrapped loop at the top of the pearl and close it securely with 2 or 3 wraps. Connect the earring hook into the top loop and repeat for the other earring.

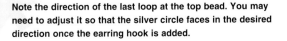

Note the direction of the last loop at the top bead. You may need to adjust it so that the silver circle faces in the desired direction once the earring hook is added.

OceanTreasure

These earrings are an artistic interpretation of the nautilus shell. Don't demand perfection from the technique here: Be playful and light-hearted with the spiral. I like the way this silver foil-lined focal bead is imperfect and slightly organic—find a focal bead that intrigues you!

30 min.

Length: 1" (3cm)

TECHNIQUES

Creating a Wire Spiral (page 24)

Creating Your Own
Earring Hooks (page 26)

Hammering (page 15)

Filing (page 15)

TOOLS

Basic Tool Kit

Earring Hook Tool Kit

MATERIALS

2 10mm silver foil-lined beads

4 5mm silver daisy spacer beads

4 2 x 3mm silver saucer spacer beads

12" (31cm) 20- or 21-gauge,
half-hard, sterling silver wire

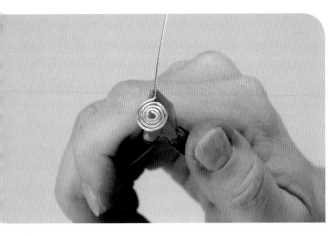

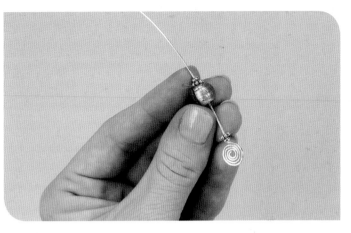

1. Create spiral and bend wire

Using the nylon-jaw pliers, straighten about 12" (31cm) of the sterling wire. Cut 2 pieces, 6" (15cm) each. Create a playful spiral about $3/8$" (1cm) in diameter at the end of the wire. If desired, gently hammer the spiral with the ball-peen end of the chasing hammer. Bend the tail up 90 degrees so it looks like a lollipop.

2. Add beads and spacers

On the long tail of the wire, slide on a silver spacer, a daisy spacer, the foil bead, another daisy spacer and a second silver spacer.

3. Create angle

Bend the wire 90 degrees perpendicular to the wire spiral.

4. Shape hook

To create the curve of the earring hook, press the angled wire against a thick-barreled pen or highlighter and wrap the wire around.

5. Cut tail and finish

Cut the tail at desired length and turn up the bottom $1/4$" (6mm) slightly. With the needle file, smooth away any sharp edges. Repeat for the second earring.

Sea**Mermaid**

Curvaceous and undeniably sensual, the unique shape of these earrings extracts the feminine qualities of the materials. The milky consistency and luster finish on the pressed glass teardrop beads mirrors the glowing, ephemeral nature of the mystical creature that inspired these earrings.

60 min.

Length: 2" (5cm)

TECHNIQUES

Creating a Wire Spiral (page 24)

Creating Your Own Earring Hooks (page 26)

Hammering (page 15)

Filing (page 15)

TOOLS

Basic Tool Kit

Earring Hook Tool Kit

Assorted Mandrels

MATERIALS

14 6mm x 9mm milky mint green pressed glass teardrop beads

16 4mm x 7mm aqua and clear mix pressed glass teardrop beads

12" (31cm) 21-gauge, half-hard, sterling silver wire

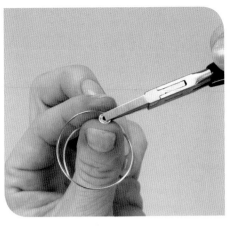

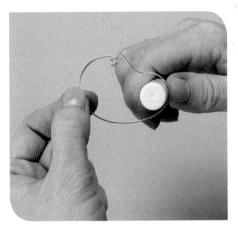

1. SHAPE WIRE

Using the nylon-jaw pliers, straighten 12" (31cm) of the sterling wire. Cut 2 pieces, 6" (15cm) each. Wrap the end of the wire around the 12 mark on a ring mandrel. It will wrap around more than once.

2. FORM SPIRAL

Create a spiral at the end of the wire. Use flat-nose pliers to assist you.

3. CREATE SHAPE

Begin to create the rounded shape of the top of the earring by gently pressing the wire between your thumb and a thick-barreled marker. Just be sure that the curve at the top has a large enough radius for the beads to slide on!

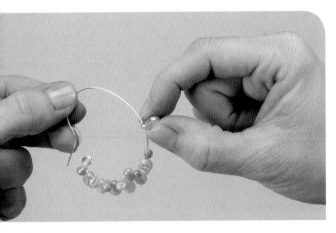

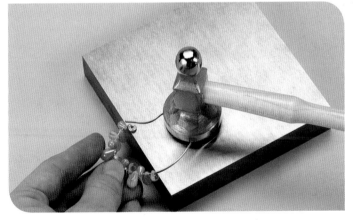

4. ADD BEADS

Once you have made both hoops, thread the glass teardrop beads onto the wire, starting with the smaller size bead and alternating with the larger drops.

5. HAMMER HOOK

Curve up the last ¼" (6mm) of wire at the end. Carefully use the chasing hammer on the exposed silver wire (avoid the beads) of the earring hook to flatten it against the steel block. This will not only work-harden the shape, but also help prevent the beads from sliding off. File the ends of the hook so they are smooth and free of sharp edges. Repeat for the other earring.

picnicinthepark

Take a deep breath in and feel the fresh air wash over you. Lie on your back and watch the drifting clouds. Watch the sun dance on the grass as it shines through the leaves on the trees. These earrings are inspired by nature, using materials and colors that exude the organic elements and rustic quality of the surrounding landscape. Be inspired by the beauty around you, wherever you are.

Deep Forest

The materials in these earrings have an organic and rich quality, reminiscent of the earth and leaves. The opacity of the dark ebony wood is in opposition to the transparency of the olivine glass briolette. The freshwater pearl in the same color palette bridges this contrast.

15 min.

Length: 1³/₄" (5cm)

TECHNIQUES

Wire Wrapping a Top-Drilled Bead with an Accent Bead (page 23)

TOOLS

Basic Tool Kit

MATERIALS

2 12mm x 12mm olivine faceted glass briolettes

2 6-7mm coordinating freshwater pearls

2 10mm x 15mm twisted ebony wood beads

4 4mm silver daisy spacer beads

6 2mm silver round spacer beads

8" (20cm) 26-gauge half-hard sterling silver wire

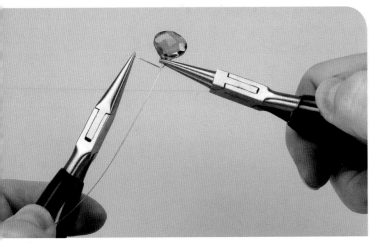

1. CUT WIRE AND WRAP BEAD

Cut 2 pieces of wire, 4" (10cm) each. Begin to wrap the briolette, leaving a long wire tail.

2. ADD BEADS

Slide a round spacer, silver daisy spacer, twisted wood bead, silver daisy spacer, round spacer, freshwater pearl and a final round spacer onto the long wire tail.

Because they're organic, freshwater pearls come in varying sizes, so try to find pearls that are close to the same size and shape.

3. CREATE CLOSED LOOP AND FINISH

Create a closed loop on top of the last spacer bead, essentially finishing the last step in Wire Wrapping a Top-Drilled Bead with an Accent Bead (page 23). Be sure to wrap the last loop in the proper direction so the earring will hang facing forward once the earring hook is added. Repeat for the other earring.

For a similar design, see **Vintage Glass Bouquet** *(page 86).*

HammeredSilverLeaf

Visually and literally lightweight, these silver leaves are geometric yet organic. The hammered texture of the silver captures the sunlight, while the faceted vessonite hints back to the lush treasures of the earth. Feel free to substitute your favorite gemstone or metal component shapes.

15 min.

Length: 2" (5cm)

TECHNIQUES

Creating a Looped Bead: Wire-Wrapped Looped Bead (page 19)

Creating a Wire Loop: Wire-Wrapped Loop (page 17)

Hammering (page 15) (optional)

TOOLS

Basic Tool Kit

Ball-Peen Hammer and Steel Block (optional)

MATERIALS

2 9mm x 21mm sterling silver leaf-shaped hoops

2 16mm x 37mm sterling silver leaf-shaped hoops

2 5mm x 8mm vessonite faceted rondelle beads

4 4mm silver daisy spacer beads

4 2mm silver round spacers

5" (13cm) 24- or 26-gauge, half-hard, sterling silver wire

2 earring hooks

1. ADD TEXTURE TO HOOPS

If desired, use the ball-peen hammer on the steel block to add texture to the sterling silver leaves.

2. INSERT HOOPS ONTO LOOP

With about 2½" (6cm) of wire, start to create an open loop. Before closing the loop, insert 1 small and 1 large leaf hoop into the loop. Close it securely with 2 or 3 wraps.

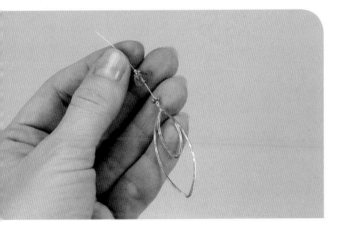

3. ADD BEADS

On the remaining wire tail, slide on a round spacer, silver daisy spacer, faceted vessonite rondelle, silver daisy spacer and another round spacer.

4. CREATE CLOSED LOOP

Create a closed loop at the top, noting that you may need to wrap the loop perpendicular to the first loop so that the earring hook will allow the earring to hang forward. Add the earring hook to the top loop and repeat for the other earring.

Vintage Glass Bouquet

These earrings are perfect for the gal who loves to score long-lost treasures at the local vintage shop. Made from vintage pressed glass beads, this design is so fresh and easy! Search for vintage beads at your recycled or vintage clothing shops, flea markets, estate sales, bead stores or at online auctions.

15 min.

Length: 1¼" (3cm)

TECHNIQUES

Wire Wrapping a Top-Drilled Bead with an Accent Bead (page 23)

TOOLS

Basic Tool Kit

MATERIALS

2 12mm x 14mm green leaf-shaped pressed glass beads

10 4mm x 7mm fuchsia AB pressed glass teardrops

7" (18cm) 24- or 26-gauge, half-hard, gold-filled wire

2 earring hooks

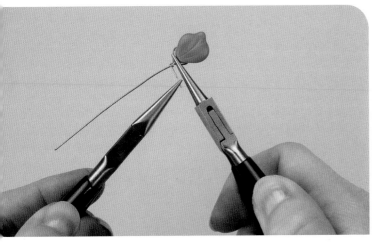

1. Wrap bead

With 3½" (9cm) of wire, wrap the top-drilled pressed glass leaf bead.

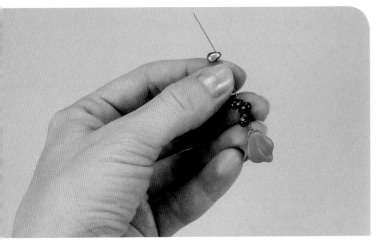

2. Add beads

Slide 5 glass teardrops onto the wire tail.

3. Create closed loop

Create a closed loop at the top, essentially finishing the last step in Wire Wrapping a Top-Drilled Bead with an Accent Bead (page 23). Be sure to wrap the last loop so that when the earring hook is added, the earring will face forward. Insert the earring hook into the top loop and repeat for the other earring.

*For a similar design, see **Deep Forest** (page 82).*

Tree Branch

When designing a jewelry piece, I take into consideration the way light reflects off of or passes through my materials. I enjoy the way these materials interact with the light: The density of the silver leaf is in contrast to the airiness of the hammered leaf outline, while the opacity of the pearls contrasts the translucency of the gemstones.

60 min.

Length: 2³/₄" (7cm)

TECHNIQUES

Creating a Looped Bead: Wire-Wrapped Looped Bead (page 19)

Creating a Wire Loop: Wire-Wrapped Loop (page 17)

Hammering (page 15) (optional)

TOOLS

Basic Tool Kit

Ball-Peen Hammer and Steel Block (optional)

MATERIALS

2 10mm x 20mm sterling silver leaf-shaped hoops

2 10mm x 15mm sterling silver leaf-shaped beads

2 5mm vessonite round beads

2 4mm green freshwater pearls

2 5mm smoky quartz faceted beads

19" (48cm) 26-gauge, half-hard, sterling silver wire

4" (10cm) sterling silver chain, delicate links

2 earring hooks

For a more organic look, hammer the sterling silver leaf hoops with the ball-peen hammer and steel block.

1. CUT CHAIN AND ADD WIRE

Cut 2 pieces of chain 1¼" (3cm) long (for the sterling hoops), and 2 pieces of chain ³/₈" (1cm) long (for the solid leaves). To wrap the silver leaf with a "vein" effect, take 4" (10cm) of wire and fold it in half around the leaf.

2. WRAP WIRE AROUND BEAD

Take the end of the wire and wrap it around the front flat side of the leaf bead, creating a "vein." Wrap 1 wire around the other at the top of the leaf 2 or 3 times to secure it.

3. ADD BEAD AND CHAIN

Slide the freshwater pearl onto the wire tail. Form an open loop and add the end of a $3/8$" (1cm) chain into the loop. Close it securely with 2 or 3 wraps. Put aside.

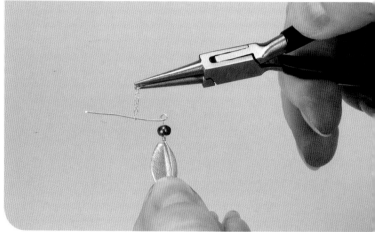

4. ADD HOOP TO LOOP

With $2\frac{1}{2}$" (6cm) of wire, create an open loop. Insert the leaf-shaped hoop into the open loop and close it securely with 2 or 3 wraps.

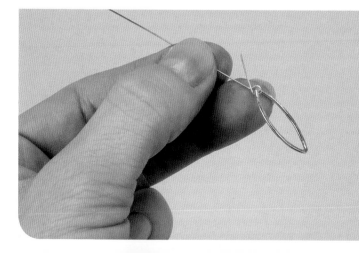

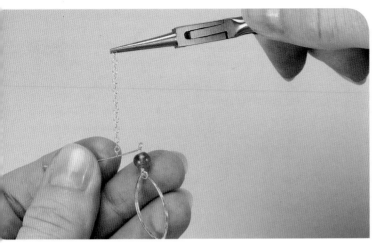

5. ADD BEAD AND CHAIN

Add a vessonite round bead onto the wire tail. Start to form the loop on top of the bead and insert the last link of a 1¼" (3cm) chain before closing. Put aside.

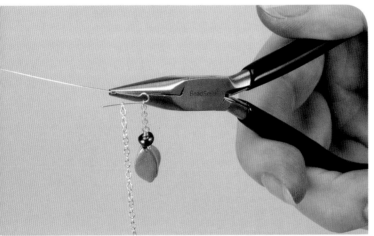

6. CREATE OPEN LOOP AND ADD CHAINS

With 2½" (6cm) of wire, form an open loop and slide in the last link of both chain segments that you have created. Close the loop securely with 2 or 3 wraps.

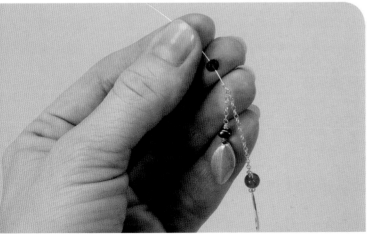

7. ADD BEAD AND FINISH

Slide the faceted smoky quartz bead onto the wire tail and close it securely with a loop on top. Add the earring hook to the top loop and repeat for the other earring.

Rose**Garden**Hoops

These earrings were inspired by my mom's resplendent rose gardens. The visual dimension of this design is heightened by the opposing color schemes, pink and green, and complementary beads of varying textures: from opaque and irregular, to sparkling and perfectly faceted, to smooth and translucent.

60 min.

Length: 2" (5cm)

TECHNIQUES

Creating your own Earring Hooks:
Hanging Wire Hoops (page 31)

Creating a Coil Wrap (page 25)

TOOLS

Basic Tool Kit

1½" (4cm) diameter mandrel

MATERIALS

16 2-3mm faceted rhodolite garnet beads

8 3mm rose AB Swarovski
round crystal beads

4 4mm fuchsia freshwater pearls

8 5mm vessonite rounds beads

12 3mm lime Swarovski round crystal beads

6 4mm olive freshwater pearls

14" (36cm) 20- or 21-gauge
half-hard gold-filled wire

40" (102cm) 26- or 28-gauge
half-hard gold-filled wire

2 earring hooks

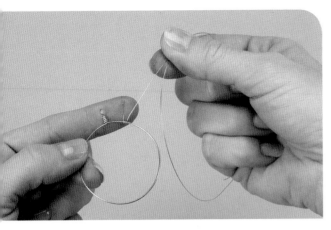

1. CREATE HOOPS AND BEGIN WIRE COIL

Create 2 wire earring hoops approximately 1½" (4cm) in diameter. You can use any round, solid object to create the diameter you want. Cut about 20" (51cm) of 26- or 28-gauge wire. At about ¾" (2cm) from the end of the wire, start to create a coil near the top of the hoop. Make 4 or 5 wraps, then push the coil you just made against the base of the wrapped loop at the top of the hoop. Cut excess wire from the short wire tail.

Make sure the wire you use to sew with will fit through the holes in all the beads you have selected.

2. ADD BEAD AND CONTINUE COIL

Once the coil is secure against the hoop, thread the first bead onto the wire. Hold the bead steady along the outside ridge, and continue winding in the same direction. Coil the wire 3 times around the hoop, or as desired.

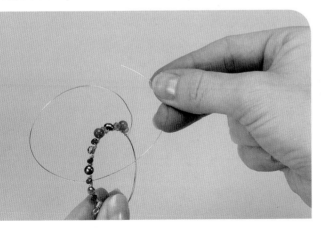

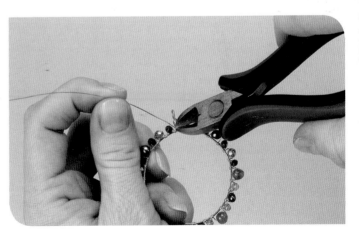

3. ADD MORE BEADS

Thread the bead in the following pattern or create your own unique pattern: (Pinks) garnet, rose, garnet, fuchsia, garnet, rose, garnet; (Greens) vessonite, lime, olive, lime. Repeat greens 2 times, add 1 vessonite. Repeat pinks.

4. WRAP AND FINISH EARRING

Continue wrapping the entire way around, and trim off any excess wire at the end. Push down any sharp ends. Add the earring hook to the top of the hoop and repeat for the second hoop.

shoppinginthecity

These earrings are *haute!* For those retail-therapy sessions on Fifth Avenue, the designs in this section are fashion-forward but not *too* trendy. The modern, geometric lines and forms are clean and timeless, yet the details add cosmopolitan flair. The simple color palettes and use of color-neutral silver beads, chain and components add to the sophistication.

Mirror, Mirror Hoops

The unusual angled facets on these silver beads create extra sparkle on these super-simple hoops. Feel free to substitute any small beads on the hoops, or alternate various bead diameters and colors. You can make any size hoop simply by changing the size of your mandrel!

30 min.

Length: 1" (3cm) diameter

TECHNIQUES

Creating your own Earring Hooks: Simple Wire Hoops (page 30)

Creating a Coil Wrap (page 25)

Hammering (page 15)

TOOLS

Basic Tool Kit

Earring Hook Tool Kit

MATERIALS

22 faceted silver beads, more or less to suit

8" (20cm) 20-gauge, half-hard, sterling silver wire (depending on hoop size)

12" (31cm) 26- or 28-gauge half-hard sterling silver wire

Make sure the holes on the beads are large enough to fit the wire used to create the hoop. Also, smaller beads will fit the curve of the earring better, so avoid long or large beads for these hoops.

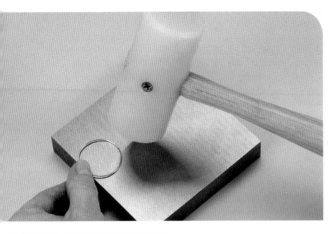

1. Create and hammer hoops

Create 2 wire earring hoops approximately 1" (3cm) in diameter. You can use just about any round, solid object to create the diameter you want. Hammer the hoops with the hard plastic mallet to work-harden the shape. (Don't bend up the last $1/4$" (6mm) of the wire yet.)

2. Add beads

Thread 11 of the faceted silver beads onto the hoop.

3. Bend wire

With the round-nose pliers, turn up the last $3/16$" (5mm) to $1/4$" (6mm) of wire that will latch inside of the other end's loop.

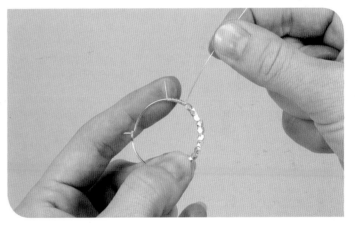

4. Create coils

With about 6" (15cm) of 26- or 28-gauge wire, begin to create a coil at an end of the set of beads. Wrap as many coils as desired, keeping in mind that you will need to leave room for your earlobe on the end that goes through your ear [about $1/4$" (6mm)]. Repeat the coil wrap on the other side of the set of beads. Repeat for the other earring.

*For more hoop earrings designs, see **Bombay Hoops** (page 64) and **Rose Garden Hoops** (page 92).*

Steel Mystique

The characteristic "blue flash" of the labradorite briolettes illuminates the otherwise monochromatic color palette of these earrings. Experiment with varying lengths and shapes of chain, as well as assorted briolettes or focal beads to create your perfect style.

15 min.

Length: 2½" (6cm)

TECHNIQUES

Wire Wrapping a Top-Drilled Bead (page 22)

Creating a Looped Bead: Wire-Wrapped Looped Bead (page 19)

TOOLS

Basic Tool Kit

MATERIALS

2 10mm x 15mm labradorite faceted briolettes

2 4mm x 7mm Montana blue Czech fire-polished rondelles

3" (8cm) sterling silver thick ladder chain

12" (31cm) 24- or 26-gauge, half-hard, sterling silver wire

2 earring hooks

1. CUT CHAINS

Determine how many chain links you would like for the desired length of earrings. Cut 2 identical length chains.

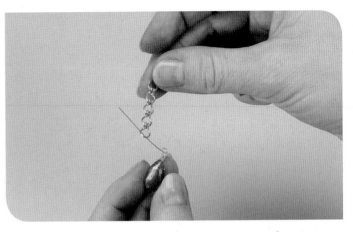

2. WRAP BEADS AND ADD CHAIN

With 3" (8cm) of wire, wrap the briolette. Before closing the loop, insert the end of a chain. Secure the loop with 2 or 3 wire wraps.

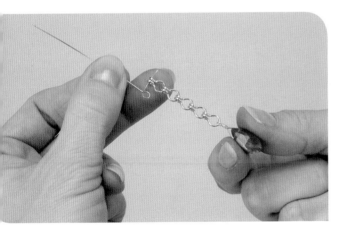

3. ADD CHAIN TO OPEN LOOP

With 2½" (6cm) of wire, create an open loop and insert the top end of the chain into the loop. Secure with 2 or 3 wire wraps.

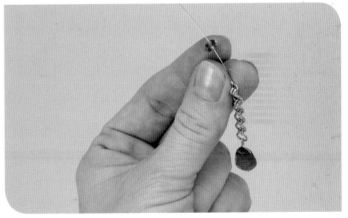

4. ADD BEAD AND CLOSE

Add the fire-polished rondelle and create a closed loop on the top of the bead. Add the earring hook to the top loop and repeat for the other earring.

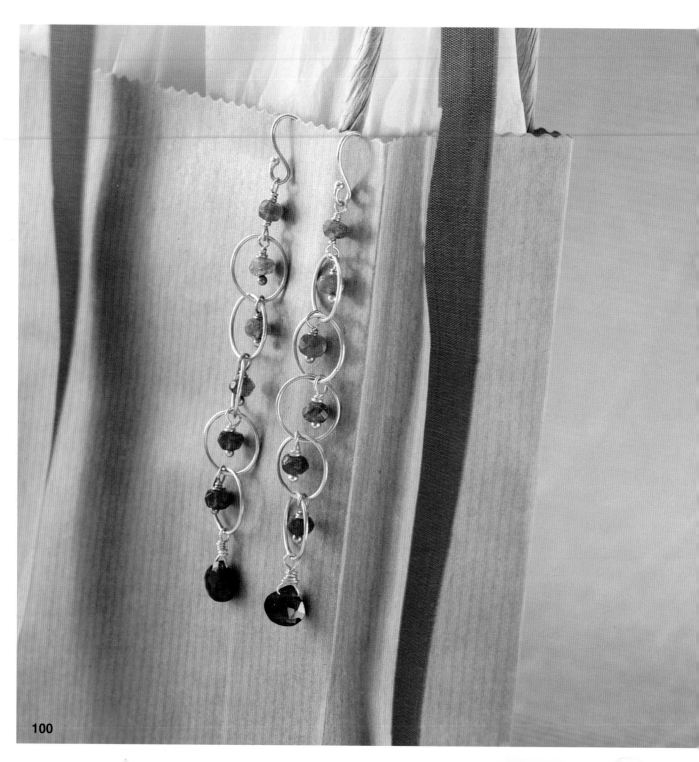

CandyRain

These earrings are so delicate: the tiny gemstones seem to drip like raindrops dancing along the thin silver circles. The subtle gradient of color from light to dark also adds to this rainfall feeling. I like using a gemstone such as tourmaline that has natural color variations for this design.

60 min.

Length: 2¹/₂" (6cm)

TECHNIQUES

Creating a Looped Bead:
Wire-Wrapped Looped Bead (page 19)

Creating a Looped Dangle:
Wire-Wrapped Looped Dangle (page 21)

Wire Wrapping a Top-Drilled Bead (page 22)

TOOLS

Basic Tool Kit

MATERIALS

2 6 x 6mm garnet faceted briolettes

12 3-4mm tourmaline faceted beads

2 segments of chain of 10mm circles, 5 segments each

10" (25cm) 26-gauge, half-hard, sterling silver wire

12 silver headpins

1. CUT CHAIN AND WRAP BEAD

Cut the circle chain into 2 equal pieces at the desired length. This design uses 5 circles [approximately 1¹/₂" (4cm)] on each earring, but feel free to lengthen or shorten as desired. Using approximately 2¹/₂" (6cm) of wire, wrap 1 of the garnet briolettes onto the bottom circle link of the chain.

2. Create and attach loop to chain

I recommend the wire-wrapped method for added durability with these delicate components. Cut 2½" (6cm) of wire and create an open loop. Before closing, add the top link of the chain into the loop. Secure with 2 or 3 wraps.

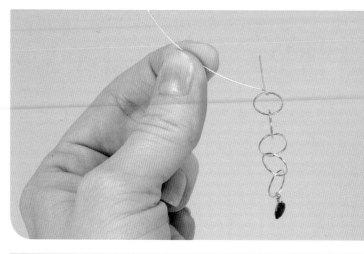

3. Add bead and close loop

Slide the rondelle onto the tail of the wire. Create a closed loop on the top. Add the earring hook. Put aside.

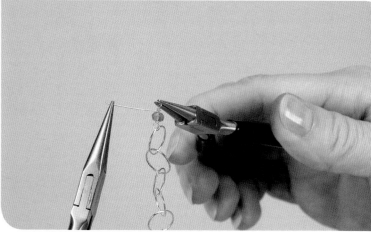

4. Create looped dangle

Thread a faceted rondelle onto a headpin and begin to form a loop. Leave the loop open.

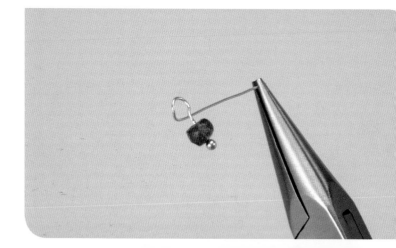

5. ADD DANGLE TO WRAPPED BEAD

Thread the dangle through the bottom loop of the wrapped bead on the earring hook.

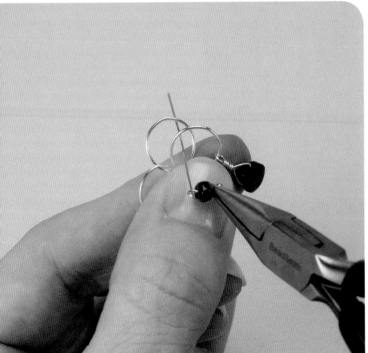

6. ADD DANGLES TO CHAIN

For the remaining dangles, slide a tourmaline bead onto a headpin and create an open loop. Slide the open loop onto the link of the chain above the link that the dangle will hang within. Close the dangle securely with 2 or 3 wraps. Repeat for the other earring.

Dynamic Hammered Teardrop

The hammered texture of these hoops provides a handcrafted touch. Yet the simplicity of the forms keeps the design very modern. Although the elements are independent from one another, the briolette on the large hoop is carefully aligned to the center of the smaller hoop below, giving this design a unified composition.

60 min.

Length: 3½" (9cm)

TECHNIQUES

Wire Wrapping a Top-Drilled Bead (page 22)

Creating a Looped Bead: Wire-Wrapped Looped Bead (page 19)

Hammering (page 15) (optional)

TOOLS

Basic Tool Kit

Ball-Peen Hammer and Steel Block (optional)

MATERIALS

2 32 x 48mm sterling silver teardrop hoops

2 20 x 30mm sterling silver teardrop hoops

2 6 x 9mm olivine cubic zirconia faceted teardrops

2 6 x 9mm peridot cubic zirconia faceted teardrops

2 4mm lime Swarovski crystal bicone beads

2 5 x 8mm olive Czech fire-polished glass rondelles

4 2 x 3mm silver saucer spacer beads

4" (10cm) sterling silver chain, delicate links (uncut, if possible)

20" (51cm) 24- or 26-gauge half-hard sterling silver wire

2 earring hooks

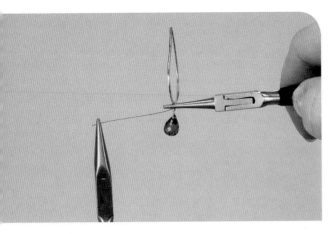

1. Hammer hoops and attach beads

If desired, hammer the sterling silver teardrop hoops to give them extra texture. With about 2½" (6cm) of sterling silver wire each, wire-wrap the olivine (or darker color) briolette to the smaller teardrop hoop and the peridot (or lighter color) briolette to the larger teardrop hoop. Repeat for the other 2 briolettes. Set these aside.

2. Create open loop and add hoop and chain

With about 2½" (6cm) of wire, begin to create an open loop and insert a smaller teardrop hoop set. Close the loop securely with 2 or 3 wraps. Slide on a 4mm lime crystal. Create an open loop on top of this crystal and insert the end of the uncut chain. Set this aside.

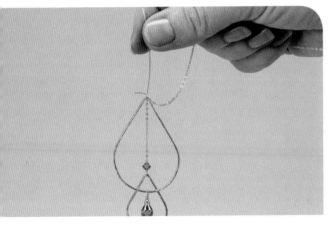

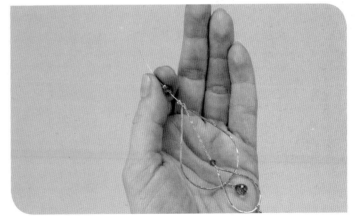

3. Attach hoops to chain

With about 2½" (6cm) of wire, begin to create an open loop and slide the larger silver teardrop hoop onto it. With some trial and error, slide the uncut chain/teardrop set from step 2 onto the open loop until you determine the length of chain you want in relationship to the larger teardrop. Once that length is determined, close the loop and cut off the remaining chain.

4. Add bead and finish

On the remaining wire tail, slide on the silver spacer, olive rondelle and silver spacer and create a closed loop on top. Add the earring hook to the top loop and repeat for the other earring.

In this project, I wanted the briolette on the larger teardrop hoop perfectly framed by the smaller silver teardrop hoop. You may need to try a variety of link lengths before determining the length you like best.

sundaybrunch
withfriends

Is there anything better than brunch at a sunny sidewalk cafe, sipping cappuccino and chatting with friends? Only doing so while looking super stylish! From sweet to spicy, the mouth-watering earrings on the following pages should whet your creative appetite. Take a fresh look at all the ingredients in your bead collection, and create something delicious!

DimSum

For those of us who prefer our brunch a little more on the savory side, spice it up with an Asian-inspired earring design! This modern interpretation is inspired by the antiques and textiles of the Far East. The detailed carving in the brilliant red faux cinnabar beads paired with the black flowers reminds me of decorative silk brocade.

30 min.

Length: 1½" (4cm)

TECHNIQUES

Creating a Looped Dangle: Wire-Wrapped Looped Dangle (page 21)

Creating a Looped Bead: Wire-Wrapped Looped Bead (page 19)

TOOLS

Basic Tool Kit

MATERIALS

2 15mm carved faux-cinnabar beads

2 3 x 5mm black Czech fire-polished glass rondelle beads

2 5 x 8mm black Czech fire-polished glass rondelle beads

4 4mm silver daisy spacers

8 8mm black pressed glass flower beads

6" (15cm) 24- or 26-gauge, half-hard, sterling silver wire

8 headpins

2 earring hooks

1. Create dangles

With the headpins and pressed glass flower beads, create 8 dangles using your preferred looping technique. Use the wire-wrapped method (shown) for a more secure dangle.

2. Create open loop and add dangles

With about 3" (8cm) of wire, start to create an open loop. Before closing the loop, slide 4 of the flower dangles onto the loop. Close it securely with 2 or 3 wraps.

3. Add beads and finish

On the wire tail, slide on the larger faceted rondelle, a silver daisy spacer, the carved bead, another silver daisy spacer, then the smaller faceted rondelle. Create a closed loop at the top. Add the earring hook and repeat for the other earring.

Paper Lantern Tassel

Like charming Japanese paper lanterns decorating a sidewalk cafe, these round wood beads are modern in form, yet traditional in style. The levity of the white globe is enhanced by the warm light streaming down the golden chain. Feel free to use other Asian-influenced beads made of wood, cloisonné or enamel.

30 min.

Length: 2½" (6cm)

TECHNIQUES

Creating a Looped Bead: Wire-Wrapped Looped Bead (page 19)

TOOLS

Basic Tool Kit

MATERIALS

2 20mm white carved wood beads

4 5mm gold cone-shaped beads

18" (46cm) gold-filled chain, delicate links

7" (18cm) 24-gauge, half-hard, gold-filled wire

2 earring hooks

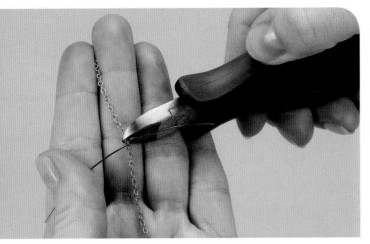

1. Cut chain

Cut the chain into 12 pieces of 1½" (4cm) lengths. Feel free to go longer or shorter, or to add more chains for a fuller tassel!

When cutting chain, especially with tiny links, I find it helpful to count out the links and slide a piece of wire in the last link to "hold my place." Not only does it mark the correct length, but it allows me to hold the chain taut when I cut the link directly above the wire.

2. Create open loop and add chains

With 3½" (9cm) of 24-gauge wire, begin to create an open loop. Before closing the loop, insert 6 of the chains into the loop and then close it securely with 2 or 3 loops.

3. Add beads and finish

Slide a gold cone bead, a white wood bead and another gold cone bead onto the wire, and then close it securely with 2 or 3 wraps. Add the earring hook to the top loop and repeat for the other earring.

*See **Red Carpet Tassel** (page 136) and **Sun and Sea Swing** (page 62) for design alternatives.*

Champagne Mimosa

Like a fizzy mimosa cocktail, these earrings are light and sweet. The warm gold tones of the metal components and crystals complement the natural iridescent shimmer of the mother-of-pearl beads.

Length: 1½" (4cm)

TECHNIQUES

Creating a Looped Dangle: Wire-Wrapped Looped Dangle (page 21)

Creating a Looped Bead: Wire-Wrapped Looped Bead (page 19)

TOOLS

Basic Tool Kit

MATERIALS

2 15mm gold circles

2 10mm mother-of-pearl coin-shaped beads

6 5.5mm golden shadow Swarovski crystal simplicity beads

6" (15cm) 26-gauge, half-hard, gold-filled wire

6 headpins

2 earring hooks

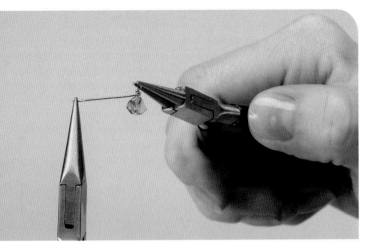

1. CREATE DANGLES

To create each dangle, slide 1 crystal onto a headpin and create a wire-wrapped loop on top. Repeat this 5 more times.

To create the dangles, I am using the wire-wrapped looped dangle technique (page 21). Feel free to use the simple looped dangle technique (page 20) to simplify the project.

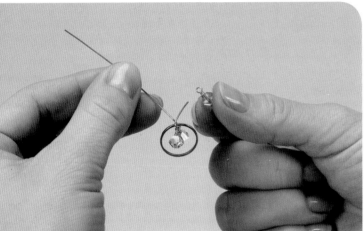

2. CREATE LOOP AND ADD DANGLES

Cut a 3" (8cm) piece of wire. Start to create an open loop. Before closing the loop, insert 3 of the crystal dangles and 1 of the gold circles. Close the loop securely with 2 or 3 wraps.

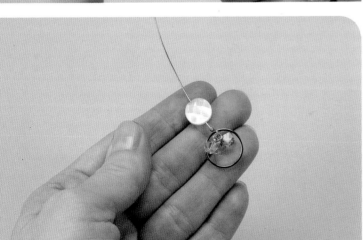

3. ADD BEADS AND FINISH

Slide the mother-of-pearl bead onto the vertical wire, and then create a loop at the top. Add the earring hook. Repeat for the other earring.

RaspberrySorbetBriolette

These tempting earrings are like a delightful dessert—assorted sweet sorbet-like shades of pink are topped with raspberry drizzle accents. Substitute your personal favorite color palette, or use contrasting crystal colors with the briolettes for a little added flavor.

30 min.

Length: 2½" (6cm)

TECHNIQUES

Wire Wrapping a Top-Drilled Bead with an Accent Bead (page 23)

Creating a Looped Bead: Wire-Wrapped Looped Bead (page 19)

TOOLS

Basic Tool Kit

MATERIALS

2 6 x 9mm briolettes, dark pink

2 6 x 9mm briolettes, light pink

2 6 x 9mm briolettes, pink

2 4mm fuschia AB Swarovski crystal bicone beads

2 4mm rose AB Swarovski crystal bicone beads

2 4mm light rose AB Swarovski crystal bicone beads

2 5 x 8mm rose quartz faceted rondelle beads

4 4mm silver daisy spacer beads

4 2mm silver round spacer beads

6" (15cm) sterling silver chain, delicate links

20" (51cm) 26-gauge, half-hard, sterling silver wire

2 earring hooks

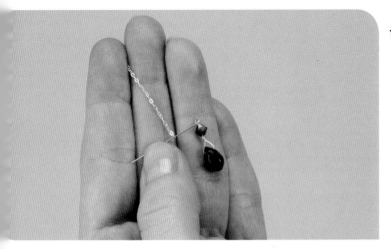

1. CUT WIRE AND WRAP BRIOLETTES

Cut your chain into 2 pieces each of short, medium and long lengths. With 2½" (6cm) of wire for each, wrap your briolettes with the coordinating accent crystals. Before you close the loop at the top, add the corresponding chain. In this design, I have paired up the chain lengths with the colors: i.e., longest chain with the darkest pink; shortest chain with the lightest pink. [See chain-cutting tip (page 111).]

Suggested lengths of chain:
Short—¼" (6mm)
Medium— ¾" (2cm)
Long—1¼" (3cm)
Experiment to find the perfect length for your beads.

2. ADD AND ARRANGE CHAINS

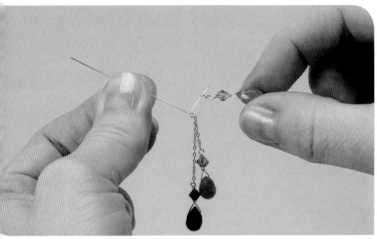

With 2½" (6cm) of wire, create an open loop. Slide on the end chain link of each of the 3 color sets onto the open loop. Arrange the strands in order of length: shortest in the front, longest in back. Close the loop securely with 2 or 3 wraps of the wire.

3. ADD BEADS AND FINISH

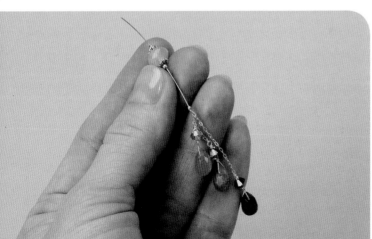

On the wire tail, slide on a silver round spacer, daisy spacer, rose quartz rondelle, daisy spacer and another silver round spacer. Create a closed loop at the top. Add the earring hook to the top loop and repeat for the other earring.

afternoonwedding

A celebration of love—an afternoon wedding in a park or garden or on the beach is the perfect occasion for darling sundresses and flowing skirts— very feminine, light and lovely. Feel free to create the following delightful earrings in colors to coordinate with your favorite special occasion dress to make a perfect match!

Garden Trellis

The ornate metalwork on these premade silver components poetically mimics the decorative gates and trellises tucked into romantic gardens. I've selected a natural-colored briolette to reinforce the theme. This raspberry jade color reminds me of wine grapes growing along trellis vines.

15 min.

Length: 3" (8cm)

TECHNIQUES

Creating a Looped Bead: Wire-Wrapped Looped Bead (page 19)

Wire Wrapping a Top-Drilled Bead with an Accent Bead (page 23)

TOOLS

Basic Tool Kit

MATERIALS

2 10 x 25mm sterling silver decorative connectors

2 10 x 15mm raspberry jade briolettes

2 6mm coordinating freshwater pearls

2 5 x 8mm raspberry jade faceted rondelle beads

4 4mm silver daisy spacers

4 2mm silver round spacer beads

11" (28cm) 26-gauge, half-hard, sterling silver wire

2 earring hooks

1. WRAP BEADS

With 2½" (6cm) of wire, wrap the raspberry jade briolette and freshwater pearl to the bottom of the decorative silver connector. Set aside.

2. ADD DECORATIVE ELEMENT

Cut 2½" (6cm) of wire and begin to create an open loop. Insert the other end of the decorative component into the loop. Close it securely with 2 or 3 wraps.

3. ADD BEADS AND FINISH

On the wire tail, slide on a 2mm spacer, 4mm daisy spacer, faceted rondelle, another daisy spacer and a second 2mm spacer. Create a closed loop at the top of the beads. Add the earring hook to the top loop and repeat for the other earring.

*See **The Essential Black Earrings** (page 134) for another variation on this design.*

Lemon**Drop**Swing

The chunkiness of this lemon quartz nugget paired with the delicate trapeze of gold chain creates a divine contrast. When you have a gemstone this luscious, sometimes it's best to keep it simple and allow the focus to be on the pure majesty of the materials.

30 min.

Length: 2½" (6cm)

TECHNIQUES

Creating a Looped Bead: Wire-Wrapped Looped Bead (page 19)

TOOLS

Basic Tool Kit

MATERIALS

2 15 x 20mm top-drilled lemon quartz nuggets

2 6mm champagne freshwater pearls

6" (15cm) gold-filled chain, decorative links

12" (30cm) 26-gauge, half-hard, gold-filled wire

2 earring hooks

1. Cut chain and add to loop

Cut 4 pieces of chain to about 1½" (4cm) each. With about 3½" (9cm) of wire, create an open loop and insert 1 end of a piece of chain within the loop. Close it securely with 2 or 3 wraps.

2. Add bead and create loop

Slide the quartz nugget onto the wire. Start to create an open loop on the other side of the nugget. Before closing the loop, slide on the last link of a second piece of chain. Close it securely with 2 or 3 wraps. Set aside.

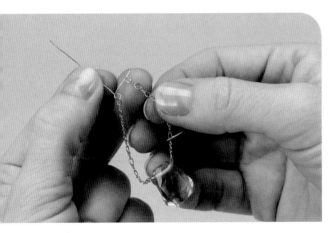

3. Create open loop and add chain

With 2½" (6cm) of wire, start to create an open loop. Slide in the last links on the 2 pieces of chain that are now creating the swing. Wrap the wire loop securely closed.

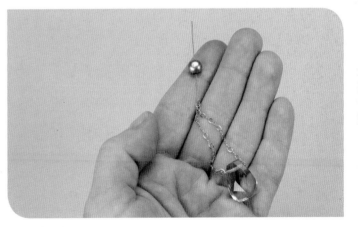

4. Add bead and finish

On the remaining wire tail, slide on the pearl and create a closed loop on the top. Add the earring hook to the top loop and repeat for the other earring.

*See **Midnight Blossom Swing** (page 139) for more design ideas using this pattern. Just a small change in the selection of beads can completely alter the look of this design!*

PrettyinPinkCluster

These earrings define romantic—they'd be a perfect match for a wedding. By graduating the pink color from dark to light, the design retains a sense of artistic organization from an otherwise eclectic collection of sparkling crystals, freshwater pearls and Czech fire-polished glass.

60 min.

Length: 2¼" (6cm)

TECHNIQUES

Wire Wrapping a Top-Drilled Bead with an Accent Bead (page 23)

Creating a Looped Dangle: Simple Looped Dangle (page 20)

Creating a Looped Bead: Wire-Wrapped Looped Bead (page 19)

Creating a Wire Loop: Simple Loop (page 16)

TOOLS

Basic Tool Kit

MATERIALS

2 10 x 11mm fuchsia Swarovski crystal briolettes

2 4mm raspberry jade faceted round beads

2 4mm fuchsia Swarovski crystal bicone beads

2 6mm fuchsia Swarovski crystal bicone beads

2 4mm rose AB Swarovski crystal bicone beads

2 6mm rose AB Swarovski crystal bicone beads

2 4mm light rose AB Swarovski crystal bicone beads

2 6mm light rose AB Swarovski crystal bicone beads

2 3 x 5mm fuchsia Czech fire-polished faceted rondelle beads

2 3 x 5mm pink Czech fire-polished faceted rondelle beads

2 3 x 5mm light rose AB Czech fire-polished faceted rondelle beads

2 4 x 8mm light rose AB Czech fire-polished rondelle beads

2 4mm dark pink pearls

2 4mm medium pink pearls

2 4mm light pink pearls

4 2mm silver round spacer beads

4 4mm silver daisy spacer beads

4" (10cm) sterling silver chain, medium links

24 headpins

2 earring hooks

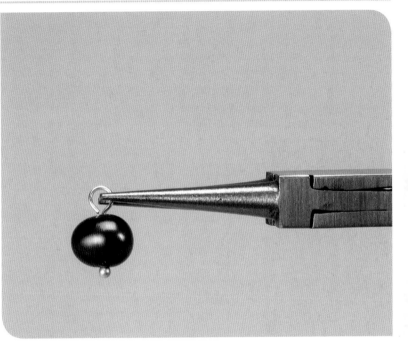

1. CREATE DANGLES

Create 2 sets of 12 matching simple looped bead dangles in assorted shades of pinks in a variety of textures and shapes. (If you opt to use the wire-wrapped technique instead, you will need to wrap the dangles directly onto the chain during step 6.)

> To create the dangles, I am using the simple looped dangle technique (page 20). Feel free to use the wire-wrapped looped dangle method (page 21) for added durability.

2. WRAP BRIOLETTE AND ADD CHAIN

With 3" (8cm) of wire, wrap the crystal briolette and faceted 4mm raspberry jade bead, and add in the last link of the uncut chain.

3. CUT CHAIN

Count 16 links and cut the chain. Set this piece aside.

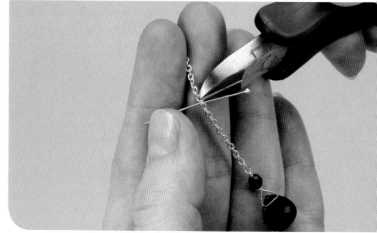

4. CREATE OPEN LOOP AND ADD CHAIN

Cut a 2½" (6cm) wire. Create an open loop. Slide on the end link of chain into the open loop. Close the loop by securing it with 2 or 3 wraps.

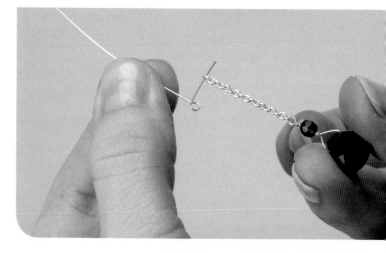

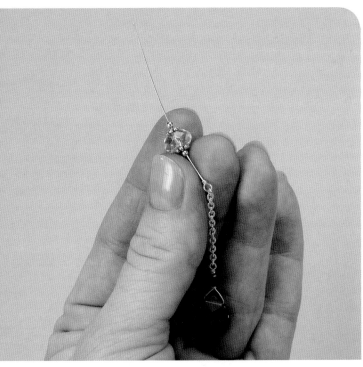

5. ADD BEADS AND EARRING HOOK

Slide a round spacer, silver daisy spacer, light rose faceted rondelle, silver daisy spacer and round spacer onto the wire tail. Create a closed loop at the top. Add the earring hook to the other end of the looped bead.

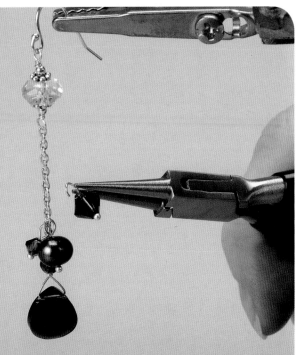

6. ADD DANGLES TO CHAIN

Start on the bottom of the chain with the darkest beads, and move up the chain with the lighter beads. Skip the first 2 links at the bottom of the chain. Start to add dangles at the third link. Add 1 dangle to each link, each time rotating the chain 1/4 turn. This will result in a spiral as you climb up the chain. Leave the last link empty, and then add 2 dangles on each side of the wire loop that is holding the top faceted rondelle bead to obtain a full, clustered look. Repeat for the other earring.

WaterfallCrystal

Can you imagine these earrings gracing your earlobes for a destination wedding on the beach? These crystals are unimaginably radiant and luminous. They gently cascade down the sterling chain like a tropical waterfall, cool and shimmering.

60 min.

Length: 2¼" (6cm)

TECHNIQUES

Creating a Looped Dangle:
Wire-Wrapped Looped Dangle (page 21)

Creating a Looped Bead: Wire-Wrapped Looped Bead (page 19)

TOOLS

Basic Tool Kit

MATERIALS

2 6 x 9mm indocolite AB Swarovski crystal teardrops beads

2 6 x 9mm aquamarine AB Swarovski crystal teardrops beads

2 6 x 9mm erinite AB Swarovski crystal teardrops beads

2 6 x 9mm peridot AB Swarovski crystal teardrops beads

2 6 x 9mm chrysolite AB Swarovski crystal teardrops beads

2 6mm Indian sapphire Swarovski crystal bicone beads

2 4mm aquamarine AB Swarovski crystal bicone beads

4" (10cm) sterling silver chain, delicate links

10" (25cm) 26-gauge, half-hard, sterling silver wire

10 headpins

2 earring hooks

It is easier to keep the chain uncut until after the dangles have been added.

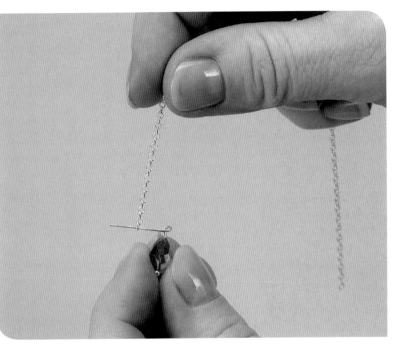

1. CREATE DANGLE AND ADD CHAIN

With the indocolite teardrop and a headpin, create a dangle and connect it to the end of the uncut chain.

2. ADD DANGLE AND CUT CHAIN

Count 5 links and add the aquamarine AB teardrop dangle. Cut chain after 3 more links. Put aside.

3. CREATE OPEN LOOP AND ADD CHAIN

With 2" (5cm) of wire, create an open loop and insert the end link of the chain with the 2 dangles attached. Close the loop securely with 2 or 3 wraps.

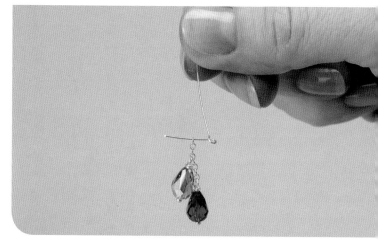

4. ADD BEADS AND CUT CHAIN

Slide a 4mm aquamarine AB bicone onto the wire tail. Begin to create an open loop and slide the uncut chain into the loop. Close it securely with 2 or 3 wraps. Count 7 links and cut the chain. Put this piece aside.

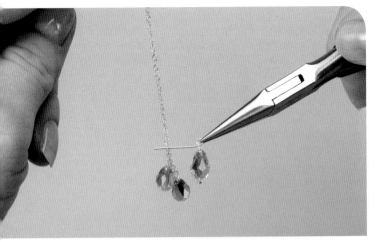

5. ADD DANGLES AND CUT CHAIN

On the uncut chain, connect an erinite AB teardrop dangle onto the last link of chain. Count 5 more links and add a peridot AB teardrop. Count 5 more links and then add the crysolite AB teardrop. Leave 1 empty link, then cut the chain.

6. CREATE OPEN LOOP AND ADD BOTH CHAINS

With 2½" (6cm) of wire, start to create an open loop. Thread the 2 crystal and chain strands from steps 4 and 5 onto the loop and close it securely with 2 or 3 wraps.

7. ADD BEAD AND FINISH

On the wire tail, slide on the 6mm bicone crystal and create a closed loop at the top. Add the earring hook and repeat for the other earring.

black-tie**evening**

Glamorous elegance is the theme for the evening. Luxurious materials, deep colors and rich blacks keep these earring designs refined and upscale. Always in vogue, these classic designs will be cherished for many years, and many special events, to come.

Timeless**Crystal**

This is a perfect example of keeping-it-simple: The focus of this piece is on the exquisiteness of the focal bead, and accent beads are used only to enhance its beauty. These understated and timeless earrings can be made in just minutes—you can use this pattern to showcase virtually any beautiful bead in your collection.

15 min.

Length: ³/₄" (2cm)

TECHNIQUES

Creating a Looped Dangle (pages 20–21)

TOOLS

Basic Tool Kit

MATERIALS

2 12mm silver shade
Swarovski crystal rondelle beads

4 4mm silver daisy spacer beads

2 2 x 3mm silver saucer spacer beads

2 headpins

2 earring hooks

1. ADD BEADS

To create the dangle, slide a silver daisy spacer, crystal rondelle, silver daisy spacer and silver saucer spacer onto a headpin.

2. CREATE LOOP

Create a loop on top of the beads, using either the simple loop or wire-wrapped technique.

3. ADD HOOK

Add the earring hook to the top loop. Repeat for the other earring—super simple!

TheEssentialBlackEarrings

Poised and polished, the decorative metal components used in this design instantly transform ordinary black beads into extraordinary baubles. These classic earrings will become a perennial favorite in your repertoire: They are perfectly comfortable with jeans, as well as a ball gown!

15 min.

Length: 1³/₄" (5cm)

TECHNIQUES

Wire Wrapping a Top-Drilled Bead (page 22)

Creating a Looped Bead: Wire-Wrapped Looped Bead (page 19)

TOOLS

Basic Tool Kit

MATERIALS

2 8 x 12mm black faceted teardrop glass beads

2 sterling silver decorative components

2 4 x 7mm black Czech fire-polished faceted rondelle beads

4 4mm silver daisy spacer beads

4 2mm silver round spacer beads

12" (31cm) 26-gauge, half-hard, sterling silver wire

2 earring hooks

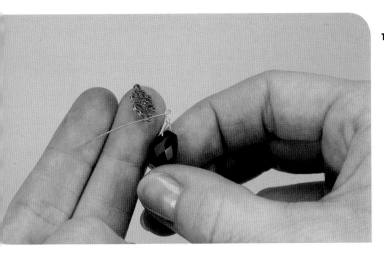

1. WRAP BEAD

With 3" (8cm) of wire, wrap the black briolette to the bottom of the decorative silver connector. Set aside.

2. CREATE LOOP

Cut 2½" (6cm) of wire and begin to create an open loop. Insert the other end of the decorative component into the loop. Close it securely with 2 or 3 wraps.

Note the direction of the top loop and adjust as necessary to ensure that the front of the decorative component is facing forward once the earring hook is added.

3. ADD BEADS AND FINISH

On the wire tail, slide on a 2mm spacer, 4mm daisy spacer, faceted rondelle, 4mm daisy spacer and 2mm spacer. Create a closed loop at the top of the beads and add the earring hook. Repeat for the other earring.

*See **Garden Trellis** (page 118) for another variation on this design.*

Red Carpet Tassel

Make a grand entrance! The playful swing of the gemstones at the ends of the sterling silver tassels adds lighthearted movement to this otherwise formal design. Feel free to substitute the faceted garnet with other gemstones such as black onyx, or use sparkling crystals instead.

Length: 2¼" (6cm)

TECHNIQUES

Creating a Looped Dangle: Wire-Wrapped Looped Dangle (page 21)

Creating a Looped Bead: Wire-Wrapped Looped Bead (page 19)

TOOLS

Basic Tool Kit

MATERIALS

14 2-3mm garnet faceted beads

2 large silver decorative beads

22" (56cm) sterling silver chain, delicate links

4 3mm silver round spacer beads

5" (13cm) 26-gauge, half-hard, sterling silver wire

14 headpins

2 earring hooks

Be sure the headpins will fit through holes of the beads and also the links on the chain.

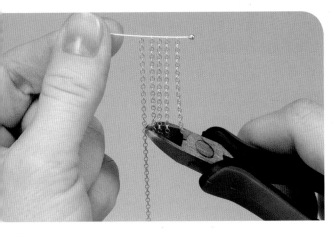

1. CUT CHAINS

Cut 14 lengths of the chain 1½" (4cm) long (count by links to ensure accuracy). Feel free to shorten or lengthen to suit your taste.

Try varying the length of the chains for a more playful and dynamic style.

2. CREATE DANGLES

To create each dangle on the tassel, insert a headpin into the faceted garnet bead, and then make a wire loop and insert the last link on the chain. Close it securely with 2 or 3 wraps. Repeat for each of the chain tassel strands.

To ensure that the dangles won't fall off the chain, I recommend using the wire-wrapped method (page 21) over the simple looped method (page 20), but feel free to use whichever method is more comfortable for you!

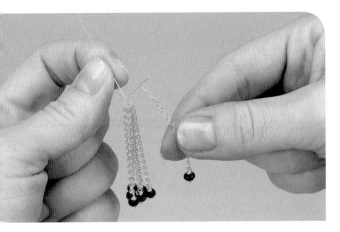

3. CREATE OPEN LOOP AND ADD CHAINS

With about 2½" (6cm) of wire, create an open loop. Insert 7 chains into the loop before closing it securely with 2 or 3 wraps.

4. ADD BEADS AND FINISH

Slide the 3mm round spacer, a large silver decorative bead and another 3mm round spacer onto the tail of the wire and make a closed loop at the top. Add an earring hook and repeat for the other earring.

See **Sun and Sea Swing** (page 62) for a variation on this design.

Midnight Blossom Swing

These dramatic earrings feature flat or "pear-shaped" teardrop faceted glass beads. A teardrop shape works best for this design because it naturally follows the curvature of the wire, but feel free to experiment with top-drilled pearls or small gemstone briolettes.

30 min.

Length: 2¼" (6cm)

TECHNIQUES

Creating a Looped Bead: Wire-Wrapped Looped Bead (page 19)

TOOLS

Basic Tool Kit

MATERIALS

10 6 x 9mm black faceted glass flat teardrops

2 5 x 8mm black Czech fire-polished faceted rondelle beads

6" (15cm) sterling silver chain, delicate links

16 2mm silver round spacer beads

4 4mm silver daisy spacer beads

12" (31cm) 24-gauge, half-hard, sterling silver wire

2 earring hooks

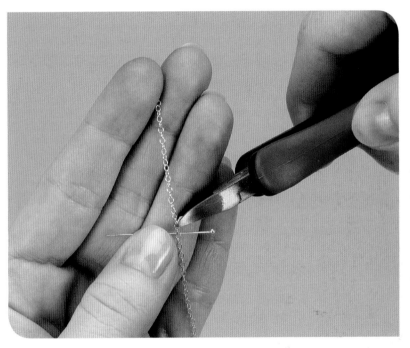

1. CUT CHAIN

Cut 2 pieces of chain to about 1¼" (3cm) each. Feel free to lengthen or shorten to suit your taste.

2. Add chain to loop

With about 3½" (9cm) of wire, create a small open loop and insert 1 end of a chain within the loop. Close it securely with 2 or 3 wraps.

3. Add beads

Slide a silver round spacer onto the wire, followed by a black teardrop. Repeat, alternating the spacers and teardrops until 6 spacers and 5 teardrops have been threaded onto the wire.

4. Create open loop and add chain

Create a small open loop on the other side of the teardrop "bloom." Before closing the loop, slide on the last link of the second piece of chain. Close it securely with 2 or 3 wraps.

5. SHAPE WIRE

Apply slight pressure to the beaded section of the wire to form the curved shape. Set aside.

6. CREATE SWING

With 2¹/₂" (6cm) of wire, start to create an open loop. Slide in the last links on the 2 pieces of chain that are now creating the swing. Wrap the wire loop securely closed.

7. ADD BEADS AND FINISH

On the vertical wire, slide on a round spacer, silver daisy spacer, faceted black rondelle, silver daisy spacer and round spacer. Create a closed loop on the top. Add the earring hook to the top loop and repeat for the other earring.

*See **Lemon Drop Swing** (page 120) for more design ideas using this pattern.*

nightonthetown

It's Saturday night and it's the perfect excuse to step into the limelight. Take this opportunity to be daring and bold. These earring designs are funky, flashy and fun, inspired by the vitality of the night lights and the energy of dancing to the rhythm until the early hours of the morning. Be dazzling!

Geometric Discotheque

Long and sleek, these earrings are deceptively simple. Select some big, bold chain and intensify the effect with a few strategically placed sparking crystal dangles.
Let the length just brush your shoulders for added opulence.

30 min.

Length: 2³/₄" (7cm)

TECHNIQUES

Creating a Looped Dangle: Simple Looped Dangle (page 20)

Creating a Looped Bead: Simple Looped Bead (page 18)

Creating a Wire Loop: Simple Loop (page 16)

TOOLS

Basic Tool Kit

MATERIALS

4 8mm black diamond Swarovski crystal round beads

2 6mm black diamond Swarovski crystal bicone beads

2 4mm black diamond Swarovski crystal bicone beads

6" (15cm) gunmetal chain with large circles

4" (10cm) 26-gauge black or gunmetal wire

6 headpins

2 earring hooks

To create the dangles and intermediate looped beads, the instructions here use the simple looped dangle technique (page 20). Feel free to use the wire-wrapped looped dangle (page 21) for added durability, as shown in the featured photograph.

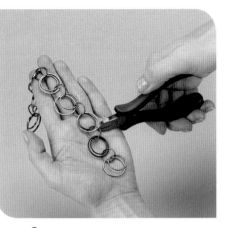

1. Create dangles

Create 2 4mm bicone crystal dangles and 4 8mm crystal dangles by sliding each bead onto a headpin and making a simple loop at the top.

2. Cut chain

Cut the circle chain into 2 pieces, each with 3 sets of circles.

3. Make simple loop and add bead

Cut a piece of wire to about 2" (5cm). Create a simple loop, slide on a 6mm bicone crystal and create a loop at the top. Make 2 of these. (For instructional purposes, I used a different colored wire for this photo.)

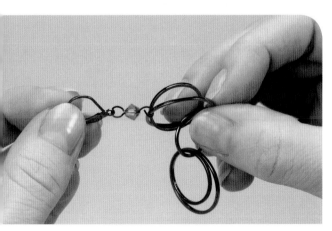

4. Add hook

Carefully open both of the loops on the piece you made in step 3. Insert the earring hook in 1 loop and close it. In the other loop, insert the cut chain from step 2, then close it.

5. Add dangles and finish

Carefully open each of the loops of the dangles from step 1 and connect the bottom bicone dangle and 2 round dangles to the chain of each earring in the pattern as shown. Repeat steps 4 and 5 for the other earring.

CityLightsCrystal

Embellish your lobes with these lovelies! Geometrically modern, yet classically constructed, these head-turners feature sparkling crystals that flirtatiously drip down the sterling silver chain. These earrings strike a perfect balance of elegance and verve.

60 min.

Length: 2¹/₄" (6cm)

TECHNIQUES

Creating a Looped Dangle: Simple Looped Dangle (page 20)

Creating a Looped Bead (page 18)

Creating a Wire Loop: Simple Loop (page 16)

TOOLS

Basic Tool Kit

MATERIALS

2 13 x 20mm silver oval hoops

18 5.5 mm silver shade Swarovski crystal simplicity beads

10" (25cm) 26-gauge, half-hard, sterling silver wire

2" (5cm) sterling silver chain, medium links

14 headpins

2 earring hooks

To create the dangles and looped beads, the instructions here use the simple looped dangle technique (page 20). Feel free to use the wire-wrapped looped dangle (page 21) for added durability, as shown in the featured photograph.

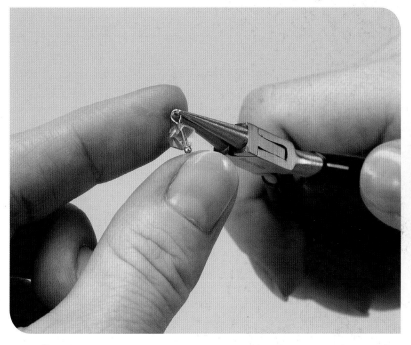

1. CREATE DANGLES

With a crystal on each headpin, create 16 bead dangles.

2. Cut chain and add to loop

Cut a piece of chain to a length of 6 links. With 2½" (6cm) of wire, begin to create a loop, and insert the last link of cut chain onto loop. Close the loop securely with 2 or 3 wraps.

3. Add bead and create loop

On the wire tail, slide on a crystal and begin to create an open loop on the top. Slide the oval metal component onto the loop before closing.

4. Create loop and add oval

Cut about 2½" (6cm) of wire and create an open loop. Before closing the loop, add the oval metal component. Close it securely with 2 or 3 wraps.

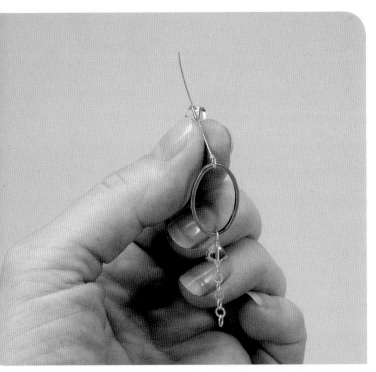

5. ADD BEAD AND EARRING HOOK

Add a crystal to the wire tail and create a closed loop on top. Add the earring hook.

6. ADD DANGLES

With the dangles you made in step 1, add 1 dangle to the end link of the chain. Skip 1 link on the chain, and then add 1 dangle to the third link. Add 1 dangle to the fourth link, on the opposite side from the link below it. On the fifth and sixth links, add a crystal dangle on both sides of the links. Repeat steps 2-6 for the other earring.

SilverExplosion

Like mini-disco balls, these flashy earrings prove they can deliver a lot of energy in a small package. Experiment with different types of beads: metallic, luster, opaque, transparent. Keep it monochromatic, or mix it up with a variety of contrasting colors and finishes.

60 min.

Length: ⁵⁄₈" (2cm)

TECHNIQUES

Creating a Looped Dangle: Simple Looped Dangle (page 20)

Creating a Wire Loop: Simple Loop (page 16)

TOOLS

Basic Tool Kit

MATERIALS

36 4mm silver metallic Czech fire-polished glass beads

6 links of silver chain with large links (at least 3mm each)

36 headpins

2 earring hooks

In this piece, keep the chain long and uncut until after the bead dangles have been attached. It makes holding the chain much easier!

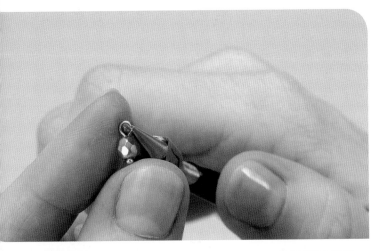

1. Create dangles

With a fire polished bead on each headpin, create 36 bead dangles.

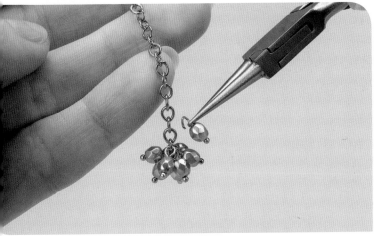

2. Add dangles

Add 8 bead dangles to the last link of each chain (or as many as will fit onto the chain link). On the second link of each chain, add 3 dangles to each side of the link.

In this design, I use the simple looped dangle (page 20), but feel free to use the wire-wrapped method (page 21) to wrap the bead dangles directly onto the chain for additional durability.

3. Cut chain and finish

On the third link, add the ear wire and then 2 more dangles on each side. Cut off the excess chain. Repeat for the other earring.

Mobility

These mesmerizing earrings dynamically rotate like a hanging mobile. The intertwined effect of the two hoops creates dimension and depth. The hammered sterling silver reflects the ambient light and draws attention to the luminous gem highlighted within the center.

60 min.

Length: 2¼" (6cm)

TECHNIQUES

Creating a Looped Bead: Wire-Wrapped Looped Bead (page 19)

Creating a Wire Loop (page 16)

Hammering (page 15)

TOOLS

Basic Tool Kit

Ball-Peen Hammer and Steel Block

MATERIALS

2 27 x 40mm sterling silver teardrop hoop

2 33 x 48mm sterling silver teardrop hoop

16" (41cm) 26-gauge, half-hard, sterling silver wire

2 17mm crystal silver shade Swarovski crystal polygon beads

2 5 x 8mm Montana blue Czech fire-polished rondelle beads

4" (10cm) sterling silver chain, delicate links

2 earring hooks

With the ball-peen hammer and steel block, hammer the sterling teardrop hoops for a sparkly, artisan feel [See Hammering (page 15)].

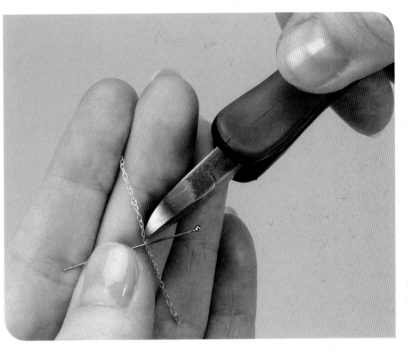

1. CUT CHAIN

To make the swing, cut 2 lengths of chain about ¾" (2cm) long. You may need to experiment with your preferred length of chain, based on the size of the individual links and your specific beads and hoops.

2. Create open loop and add chains

With 3" (8cm) of wire, start to create an open loop. Make it as small as the pliers will allow. Before you close the loop, slide the end link of 1 of the chains, that you cut in step 1 into the loop. Close the loop securely with 2 or 3 wraps of the wire.

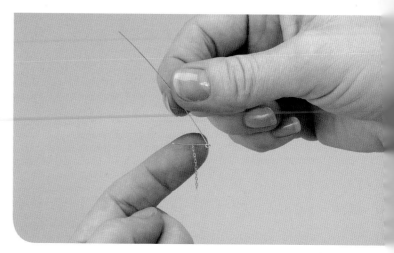

3. Add bead and chain

Slide the briolette onto the wire tail, and then begin to make another loop as small as possible. Slide the end link of the second chain into the loop before closing it. Wrap it securely. Set this aside.

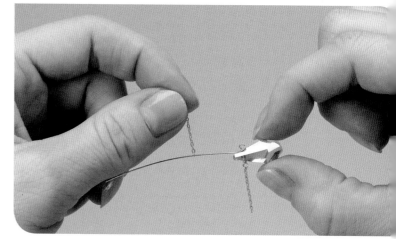

4. Create open loop and add beads and chain

With about 2½" (6cm) of wire, create an open loop. Slide on the last links of the 2 chains that are holding the polygon crystal and the smaller teardrop hoop. Close it securely with 2 or 3 wraps of the wire.

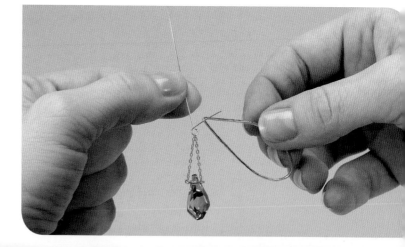

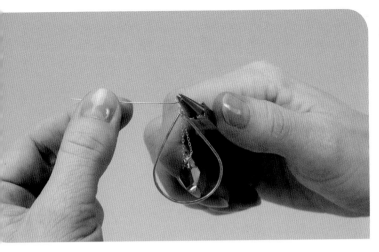

5. CREATE OPEN LOOP

In order to create a full swing effect for these earrings, create another open wire loop perpendicular to and directly on top of the one you just completed. This allows the second larger sterling teardrop hoop to swing independently of the smaller one.

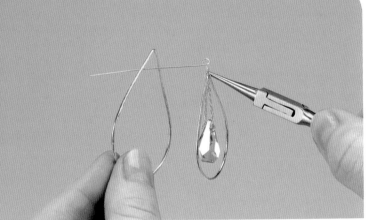

6. ADD HOOP

While the loop is open, slide the second teardrop into the loop. Close it securely by wrapping directly over the wraps from the first teardrop.

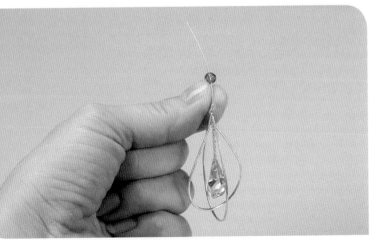

7. ADD BEAD AND FINISH

You may add the earring hook directly onto the larger teardrop at this point. Or, if you prefer more swing and length, you can add another wire-wrapped bead between the hoops and the earring hook. Repeat for the other earring.

Resources

For more resources, please visit www.PerfectMatchEarrings.com.

Beads and Pieces
Terrific selection of unusual beads
of shell, wood and bone.
www.beadsandpieces.com

Beadsmith
Affordable and reliable
jewelry-making tools.
www.beadsmith.com

Bella Findings
Large selection of crystals, chain
and wire.
www.bellafindings.com

etsy.com
Phenomenal source to buy and sell
handmade goods of every variety,
as well as purchase from a dizzying
selection of supplies.
www.Etsy.com

eBay.com
Endless options for amazing beads and
materials. Addicting!
www.ebay.com

Fire Mountain Gems
Massive selection of beads, findings,
supplies, tools and more.
www.firemountaingems.com

Halstead Beads
Silver and gold-filled wire, lots of
findings and chain.
www.halsteadbead.com

Metalliferous
Silver and gold-filled wire, decorative
components, sterling hoop shapes, tools.
www.metalliferous.com

Shipwreck Beads
Huge color selection of Czech fire-
polished glass beads and much more.
www.shipwreckbeads.com

Wig Jig
Wire jigs, tools and more. Tons of les-
sons and patterns on Web site.
www.wigjig.com

Index

Check out these other inspiring jewelry titles from North Light Books

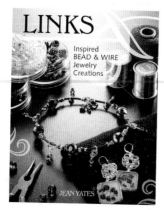

Links

By Jean Yates

Learn how to design and create beautiful jewelry filled with personal meaning. *Links* is filled with more than 35 fabulous step-by-step jewelry projects, including bracelets, necklaces, earrings and pins. Author Jean Yates explains the inspiration behind each piece and shows you how to create your own personalized variations of these unique jewelry designs. Find added inspiration in quotes from working jewelry artists and kick-start your designs with creative challenges from the author.

ISBN-13: 978-1-60061-016-5
ISBN-10: 1-60061-016-1
Paperback, 128 pages, Z1078

Bead on a Wire

By Sharilyn Miller

Magazine editor and popular author Sharilyn Miller shows crafters of all levels how to get in on the popularity of jewelry and beading. Inside *Bead on a Wire*, you'll find an in-depth section on design and construction techniques that make it a snap to get started. You'll love to make the 20 step-by-step bead and wire jewelry projects, including gorgeous earrings, necklaces, brooches and bracelets. You'll be amazed at how easy it is to start making fashionable jewelry that's guaranteed to inspire compliments.

ISBN-13: 978-1-58180-650-2
ISBN-10: 1-58180-650-7
Paperback, 128 pages, 33239

Simply Beautiful Beaded Jewelry

By Heidi Boyd

Author and designer Heidi Boyd has filled this fabulous jewelry book to the brim with more than 50 gorgeous beaded necklaces, bracelets, earrings and accessories. Her trademark style shines in each of the projects and variations. Best of all, every piece is simple to make and beautiful to wear. Even a beginning crafter can easily finish any project in the book in one afternoon. The book includes a helpful techniques section and insightful tips scattered throughout.

ISBN-13: 978-1-58180-774-5
ISBN-10: 1-58180-774-0
Paperback, 128 pages, 33445

These and other fine North Light Books are available at your local craft retailer, bookstore or online supplier, or visit our Web site at www.mycraftivity.com.